WHAT IF IT'S ALL TRUE?

"Whoever has ears to hear, let them hear."
(LUKE 8:8B)

"God either exists or he doesn't. The Bible is either God's Word, or it's not. Jesus was raised from the dead, or he wasn't. Christianity is true or it isn't. There is no 'my truth' when it comes to God."[1]

INVESTIGATING THE PERSON
AND PROMISES OF JESUS

WHAT IF IT'S ALL TRUE?

RICK BECKWITH

B&H
PUBLISHING
BRENTWOOD, TENNESSEE

This book is dedicated to my partner of thirty five years, my wife, Kris. Thank you for loving and standing with me on this wild ride. You're the best!

Contents

Contents

Foreword

Rick Beckwith is a dear family friend. He was the Young Life leader in our high school in northern Virginia and invested deeply in Pat's and my two sons, JD and Coy. The impact Rick's life and character had on our boys and so many of their peers continues to reverberate today, now over three decades later.

When I coached in Washington, we looked for the best athletes who were willing and able to fill any role necessary to benefit the team. Rick Beckwith is similar to those players. He is not an author; this is his first book. But through his forty years of working with adolescents and training leaders, Rick has gained a deep understanding of life and how it is meant to be lived. He also has forged a deep personal relationship with Jesus Christ, and now he is filling an important role to all of our benefit by sharing his insights in this book.

At one time or another we have all asked the same question: "What if it's all true?" If Jesus of Nazareth truly was God in the flesh, what implications does that have for your life and those you love? How we answer this pivotal question will affect the outcome of our lives—our thinking, words, actions, and relationships—more than any other question. I believe it is the most important question we all face regardless of age, stage of life, or previous religious involvement. You are wise to explore *What If It's All True?*

Joe Gibbs
Three-time Super Bowl–winning coach of the Washington Redskins and five-time championship owner of the Joe Gibbs Racing NASCAR team—the only person ever to be inducted into both the Pro Football and NASCAR Halls of Fame

A Note from the Author

Thank you for being willing to explore one of life's most important questions: What if it's all true? I know you will enjoy this short journey, and I hope you will be encouraged by your own conclusions.

In the face of many distorted views on His identity, Jesus asked His disciples, "Who do you say I am?" Peter answered, "You are the Messiah, the Son of the living God." Jesus then blessed him and affirmed his correct response (Matt. 16:15–17). I trust this book will be a help to you in answering this most important life question.

This book is written for you and each individual who will read it. However, it can also be explored by a small group who wishes to discuss it along the way. Questions are included at the end of each chapter for that purpose.

Now, jump in, and happy exploring!

INTRODUCTION

Weighing the Odds

Once when Jesus was alone with His disciples, He asked them, "'Who do people say the Son of Man is?' They replied, 'Some say John the Baptist; others say Elijah; and still others, Jeremiah or one of the prophets.' 'But what about you?' he asked. 'Who do you say I am?'" (Matt. 16:13–15). How important do you think our answer to this question is?

Listen to Peter's answer and how he was rewarded for getting Jesus's identity right: "Simon Peter answered, 'You are the Messiah, the Son of the living God.' Jesus replied . . . 'I tell you that you are Peter, and on this rock I will build my church, and the gates of Hades will not overcome it. I will give you the keys of the kingdom of heaven; whatever you bind on earth will be bound in heaven, and whatever you loose on earth will be loosed in heaven'" (vv. 16–19).

What Are We Wagering

It seems today we can't turn on the television or radio without hearing an ad for online betting of some sort. Sports gambling apps are all the rage for a variety of reasons. We play the odds with most decisions we make. We might think, "If I get good grades, the odds are good I will get into college." "If I time the stock market just right, I will profit. "If I use a rope when rock climbing, I will likely not die if I fall." You get the picture.

Who in their right mind would risk a million dollars for the chance to win only five dollars more? That would be a preposterous bet. However, if the Bible is true, then countless people today are wagering billions of years in eternity for just a few here. They risk losing everything on the odd chance they might be right about what awaits them after death. Not only that, but the Bible promises a life of fulfillment, meaning, and purpose here and now. So, to ignore what it says is wagering against God and billions of people who have gone before us.

If you were the oddsmaker, on which side of these propositions would you place your wager?

The Bible is a book of myths written by men.	←——→	The Bible is the inspired Word of God with relevance that transcends time.
Jesus of Nazareth was a prophet and wise teacher, but no more.	←——→	Jesus of Nazareth was truly God's Son and with Him in Creation, making Him the ultimate authority on life.

When we consider the consequences of this gamble, falling off a cliff while rock climbing seems like small potatoes. The French philosopher Blaise Pascal made a famous wager. He argued that a rational person should live as though God exists because of the benefits to them personally, as well as to society at large. Here is my interpretation of his reasoning:

- If God does not exist and we live as if He does, we have nothing to lose and much to gain by being a moral contributor to those around us.
- If God does exist and we live as if He does not, we have everything to lose—not only in this life but in eternity.
- If God does exist and we embrace Him, we have nothing to lose and everything to gain by following Him through this life and into eternity.

So what happens if it is all true, but we wager it is not? We experience a life separated from God and our very purpose. We live separated from God's blessing upon relationships, marriage, and children. We make decisions based only on what we think is best from our limited experience relative to the knowledge of an infinite God. And, in eternity, we find ourselves separated from God, His goodness, light, and life.

This is why the title of this book asks the most important question we will ever pose, and we must answer it personally, because no one else's conclusion is sufficient for our outcome. As we explore this notion together in the pages that follow, I do not ask you to check your convictions at the door. On the contrary, I merely encourage you to sift through these chapters with a keen mind open to fresh input.

Truth is rarely discerned in one sitting; it unfolds as our experiences inform us along the way. Jesus said, "Ask, and it will be given to you; seek, and you will find; knock, and it will be opened to you. For everyone who asks receives, and the one who seeks finds, and to the one who knocks it will be opened" (Matt. 7:7–8 ESV). Let's do some honest seeking together!

1

What If It's All True?

My friend Brent has lived a moral, respect-worthy life. He runs a company and cares for his employees well. He chairs the board of a charity that helps find transitional housing for the homeless. He has been faithful to his wife and provided his children with top-level educations. He is a blessing to his friends and community. But, when asked about the role of faith in his life, Brent replied, "I guess I really haven't given religion much focus."

Is it possible for us to have checked so many of the "right" boxes in life but missed the most important one? John, one of the disciples who walked the longest with Jesus, famously said, "And this is the testimony: God has given us eternal life, and this life is in his Son. Whoever has the Son has life; whoever does not have the Son of God does not have life" (1 John 5:11–12). Could Brent be missing out on life altogether? Has his very purpose in life eluded him, at least to this point?

If the Bible truly is the words of God written down by the hands of men and the primary means by which a loving God chose to show His precious creation the way to a relationship with Him, then it cannot be just another thing to which we haven't given much thought. The good news about Jesus presented in the Bible is either the path to a full and abundant life (John 10:10) or it is worth refuting so others might not also waste their time pursuing it. It must be excitedly accepted or readily refused. There is no middle ground.

I find it interesting to note that the people who encountered Jesus in His day strongly reacted to Him in one of two ways: either they were captivated by His wisdom and acts of caring and were convinced He was indeed the Son of God, or they feared He was a threat to their way of life, so they sought to kill Him. They either surrendered their life to following Him or committed their life to ending His. No one was indifferent to Him.

My, how times have changed over the last two thousand years! It is not unusual today for folks to shrug their shoulders when asked who Jesus is, as if knowing the answer is of little concern.

The Bible tells us that Jesus is either the rock upon which we can build the foundation of our lives—our chief cornerstone—or He is the rock that will crush us if we reject Him (Matt. 21:42–44). He is one or the other, but not neither. People who think the author of life can merely be an acquaintance who doesn't affect their daily lives are misunderstanding His instruction. The consequences of this are far too great to be ignored!

Oh, that we would explore Jesus sufficiently to determine for ourselves which of these two responses to Him is reasonable today! If Jesus is who He claimed to be, and who billions have followed since, we cannot naïvely relegate Him to an almost-forgotten, ancient figure.

Near the end of Jesus's life on earth some Greeks (non-Jews) approached Jesus's disciples and said they would like very much "to see Jesus" (John 12:21). "If we could only get to know Jesus ourselves, our wondering would be quenched," they surmised. Wouldn't you like to join these conscientious seekers? Who wouldn't want to have a personal encounter with the One around whom time itself is measured, the One whose presence shaped the world more than any ruler or king? If it's all true, then our lives will never be the same once we come to understand Him.

> "You see, God loved the world so much that he gave his One and Only Son, so that every single individual, whoever! Who is entrusting oneself to him would never be destroyed, oh no! but would even now have a deep, lasting life!"[2]

Discuss and Reflect

1. What are the risks of Brent's reply, "I guess I really haven't given religion much focus"?

2. Is it reasonable to believe Jesus is who He claimed to be yet not to follow Him today? Why or why not?

3. Who do you say Jesus is?

2

What Do You Seek?

"But seek first his kingdom and his righteousness,
and all these things will be given to you as well."
(MATTHEW 6:33)

Tell me this: If you could have coffee with any of your heroes, past or present, who would you choose? A sports star, famous musician, past president . . . ? I have a long list I would love someone-on-one time with, but William Wilberforce may be at the top. Wilberforce was a British politician and philanthropist who, in the late 1700s, led England and its colonies in the abolishment of the slave trade. What a world-changing accomplishment! I would love to glean insights as to how he convinced a conservative white legislature to see the injustices so deeply imbedded in their way of life. The world is certainly in need of moral reformation today on a parallel scale.

What if there was someone with wisdom for our lives, and for all mankind, beyond that of any hero? What if the Creator of the universe were to offer you not only coffee, but the privilege to walk with Him each and every day—to gain wisdom and insight regarding your vital relationships, your work, your pastimes, your very existence? How would that appeal? This is what Jesus offers all who would trust Him: "Come to me, all you who are weary and burdened, and I will give you rest. Take my yoke upon you and learn from me, for I am gentle and humble in heart, and you will find rest for your souls" (Matt. 11:28–29).

When we personally consider the question "What is it we want in life?" some consistent staples of the human existence come to mind: loving relationships, healthy families and friends, meaningful labor, a fulfilling life, authentic community. We all share these desires and perhaps others, but where we differ is in what we place our hope for achieving these ends.

"What do you seek?" is the first question Jesus posed to His first two inquiring disciples as recorded in the Gospel of John (1:38a NASB1995). These two men quickly responded: "Where are You staying?" (v. 38b NASB1995), showing how desperately they wanted to be with Jesus, wherever He was going. They had previously been disciples of John the Baptist, who was preparing his hearers for the coming of the long-prophesied Messiah.

Notice how Jesus checks these boxes held for the true Messiah:

❏ Be a visible, human expression of the invisible God (Col. 1:15)
❏ Bring an awareness of God to all people (Heb. 8:11)
❏ Pay the penalty for our sins so we can enjoy the life God intends for us, both here and in eternity (1 Pet. 3:18)
❏ Be resurrected after three days to conquer sin and offer any who would follow Him eternal life (Luke 18:33)
❏ Usher in the kingdom of God (Mark 1:15)

If it was all true, from whom else would these young disciples rather learn?

Are You Seeking Success or Fulfillment?

Harvard professor Todd Rose wrote a book in 2018 titled *Dark Horse: Achieving Success through the Pursuit of Fulfillment*. Rose's research found that Dark Horses, those from whom few expected great results, "are people who prioritize personal fulfillment over conventional notions of success. This priority is what allows these people to be both successful and happy."[3]

Dictionary.com defines success as "the favorable or prosperous termination of attempts or endeavors; the accomplishment of one's goals."[4] Our experience, and that of the most "successful" people around us, confirms that success is a short-lived experience. Once we terminate one endeavor, we move on to the next goal upon which we have set our sights. There is never a point where one is satisfied at their present state. So, it is safe to say that success has an appetite that is never quenched. Success seems as though it will lead to contentment, but it's never enough.

Scientists from the University of Queensland found that wealthy people desire more wealth and status even when they appear set for life. Professor Jolanda Jetten, coauthor of the study, submits that wealthy people, because they tend to define themselves by their wealth and status, have a continual thirst and striving to gain even more wealth and status.[5] Furthermore, her project showed those with wealth define themselves by their possessions and experienced greater identity threat when at risk of losing it.

Fulfillment, on the other hand, refers to an inner state of being that is disconnected from any outward trappings. It doesn't require riches, prestige, or promotion. Instead of feeling successful, fulfilled people feel satisfied, even joyous with who and where they are in life. You may be one of these people, but if not, I suspect you know someone who fits this description.

In Mark 10:17–31 Jesus is approached by a man only identified as a rich young ruler. Outwardly, it would appear this man would be the envy of us all—he was young, rich, and powerful. But the question he runs up to Jesus to ask reveals a different reality: "Good teacher, . . . what must I do to inherit eternal life?" (v. 17b). Essentially, he was asking Jesus what would satisfy the desire in his soul for his life to count, to be fulfilled. Jesus tells this young man that he should sell his possessions—those things he was counting on to satisfy him, and invites this man to come follow Him. The man goes away disappointed, unwilling to lay down what he believes will bring fulfillment for the One who brings it truly and eternally.

We find ourselves chasing after so many whims that won't truly fulfill: a new, better paying job; the best car or boat or house; the perfectly behaved children; the next achievement. It leaves us feeling empty, always wanting more and never arriving. Like the rich young ruler, we walk away disappointed, clinging to what is temporary rather than releasing our grip so that we might cling to One who is eternal.

The writer of the book of Hebrews refers to Jesus as "the author and perfecter" of our faith (Heb. 12:2 NASB1995), and He is the same for our lives. No one could possibly know us better. If this is true, then who better than Jesus to walk with us in our search for life?

Discuss and Reflect

1. If you could have coffee with any of your heroes, past or present, who would you choose and why?

2. What do you seek? What do you really want out of life? Who has the ability to best help you fulfill these desires?

3. Can you identify anything that holds you back from trusting Jesus with your life?

3

What Is Your Purpose?

I went to a college where 80 percent of the students joined a fraternity or sorority, as that was about the only social life available in this small Midwestern town. In my frat, we were considered a pledge for a semester before attaining full membership. Poor pledges get no respect! One night while studying in my dorm, four hooded men kidnapped and blindfolded me, threw me in the back of a pickup truck, and drove around for what seemed like an eternity. Then they pushed me out of the truck to fend for myself. It was midnight and pitch-dark in what seemed to be the middle of nowhere. There were no lights or houses in view. Cell phones had not yet been invented. I had no idea where I was or how to get back to school, so I just started walking, feeling for the edge of the road with my foot so as not to stumble off to the side. I had never seen such darkness.

I suspect you resonate with the desire to know where you are and where you are going, whether that is in the middle of the night on a dark road or in the trajectory of your life. You'll have to keep reading to hear how my story that night ended, but it's a feeling we can all understand. We want our lives to thrive and count for something bigger than ourselves, not to waste years running around lost. We desire to leave a legacy of appreciated deeds that will be recalled at our funeral. We want purpose, *real* purpose, in the direction of our lives.

Jesus offers a promise to all people if they are willing to take Him up on it. He says, "I am the light of the world. Whoever follows me will never walk in darkness, but will have the light of life" (John 8:12). When we walk in darkness, we can't see what is ahead. We stumble, get off course, and often run into barriers. These are consequences of trying to find our own way without guidance from the only one who has seen the road ahead. When lost in the dark, it is good news to see a bright light shining on our path. Jesus is called the Light of Lights, and He is the one who can pull us out of the darkness. It's in this light that our lives have purpose, and in the guidance of God that we find it.

Eric Liddell, the Scottish sprinter featured in the film *Chariots of Fire* who later became a missionary to China, explained to his sister in a famous scene: "I believe God made me for a purpose, for China, but He also made me fast, and when I run I feel His pleasure." That is how it feels to follow our purpose—we run with pleasure and feel God smiling and cheering us on! Have you experienced this feeling?

Surveys confirm that most people believe their lives have a purpose, but according to a 2018 *New York Times* study, only 25 percent of Americans say they know what that purpose is.[6] That means 75 percent are left wandering aimlessly without even a picture of what can make their lives feel truly meaningful. What about you—are you confident in your purpose? Why are you here?

It would be ill-advised to put too much stock in a purpose we invent ourselves. Most likely it would be hit-or-miss with frequent changes based on what we are experiencing at the time. To be confident in our purpose requires a belief that our purpose is assigned by one with authority, someone greater than us. Those serving in the military submit to an assigned purpose, a great and noble calling. They don't have to wonder about their purpose while enlisted; it is to serve and protect the homeland at all costs. These noble men and women gladly submit to the orders of their commanding officers because it would be disastrous if each soldier determined their own course of action. Members on a sports team function in a similar way; they follow the playbook as a united body (at least the best ones do!). This allows for sound execution and teammates who understand what it is they should be doing. A coach or an officer holds authority because of their experience or skills. They are in charge because they deserve to be.

Likewise, God holds all authority because He created all things; because He created all things, He knows how the world best works. He gives purpose to everything He has created, and when we follow in His purpose, the world looks more and more like the promised city to come. God has given you a purpose that reflects His character and brings Him glory, and surrendering to Him is the way to obtain it.

The Bible teaches that we are not accidents, but the result of an intentional Creator. King David wrote: "I praise you because I am fearfully and wonderfully made; your works are wonderful, I know that full well" (Ps. 139:14). If we are God's children, doesn't He have the authority to assign purpose to our lives? If we are merely the result of a cosmic coincidence, an accident of nature, then we neither matter in this life nor in eternity. "Eat, drink, and be merry, for tomorrow we die!"[7] Our lives would not have any intrinsic value or inherent purpose.

While frustrating circumstances can discourage us for a time, deep down we know (or at least hope) that we are the product of a skillful and loving Creator. Just as every vote counts in an election, every life matters. We matter to our families, our neighbors, our communities, and we would be sorely missed if we weren't here. There are days we may not feel like we add value to anyone, but if we were to interview the people in our inner circles, they would likely refute those thoughts. If we are God's unique handiwork, then we matter to Him as well. That is a truth that brings significance to our lives here and now, and in eternity!

What Does the Creator Say Regarding Our Purpose in Life?

Listen to what the Old Testament prophet Jeremiah reveals about God's purposes for us: "'For I know the plans I have for you,' declares the LORD, 'plans to prosper you and not to harm you, plans to give you hope and a future. Then you will call on me and come and pray to me, and I will listen to you. You will seek me and find me when you seek me with all your heart'" (Jer. 29:11–13). This was written to God's people who were exiles in Babylon, and it was not a happy time for them. Yet, even in their struggles, God was making a way for them to prosper and thrive. In His great purposes, this wouldn't be an immediate fix, but He was working on their behalf. God wants us to prosper and thrive, but likely not the prosperity we immediately consider. Prosperity for those in Christ looks like hope. It's being filled with joy and conformed to the image of Christ as we walk in the ways God has established for us. Prosperity is living as those who know that only in God is true life found.

Once, a lawyer asked Jesus the meaning of life, our purpose. He phrased his inquiry this way: "Teacher, which is the greatest commandment in the Law?" (Matt. 22:36). In other words, if we could give ourselves to the pursuit of just one noble objective, what should it be? Jesus replied: "'Love the Lord your God with all your heart and with all your soul and with all your mind.' This is the first and greatest commandment. And the second is like it: 'Love your neighbor as yourself.' All the Law and the Prophets hang on these two commandments" (vv. 37–40).

Most religious scholars confirm this is indeed the purpose for our existence: to know and love God, and to love our neighbor as we love ourselves. Clearly, this purpose is impossible for anyone to accomplish on their own. It requires divine intervention, which is exactly what Jesus offers every person who commits to follow Him. These words of Jesus in Matthew 22 are called "The Greatest Commandment." What is Jesus saying here?

First, to love God with all that we are means believing Jesus is who He claimed to be: God's Son—God who took on flesh, sent to earth so we could observe what He is like, fall in love with His character, and come to follow Him. God sent Jesus to redeem us from the weight and penalty of our sin and invites us to walk with Him in a personal relationship, from here to eternity. Second, it means trusting Jesus with our lives, by committing to follow what He says is right and best and yielding to His authority rather than doing what seems right in our own eyes.

It is when we get personally in touch with the love of Jesus that we are free to love others generously as well. This latter love flows from the former, our first love. And when we come to grasp how much God loves us, we are better equipped to love ourselves. Without this knowledge we will likely always struggle with our identity and self-esteem.

The apostle Paul summarizes this posture in his letter to the Galatians: "I have been crucified with Christ and I no longer live, but Christ lives in me. The life I now live in the body, I live by faith in the Son of God, who loved me and gave himself for me" (Gal. 2:20). Living by faith does not mean knowing all the answers or understanding God's mind completely. It means trusting that Jesus is who He says He is, and that our thriving is His priority. It means believing Jesus when He says, "I came that [you] may have life and have it abundantly" (John 10:10 ESV).

Once, after feeding a crowd of more than five thousand with just five loaves of bread and two small fish, some in this enthusiastic crowd of onlookers shouted to Jesus, "What must we do to do the works God requires?" Jesus replied, "The work of God is this: to believe in the one he has sent" (John 6:28–29). If we put our belief in Jesus, He promises to give our lives meaning and purpose. Every important aspect of our lives will be impregnated by that belief and give birth to meaning, peace, and out-of-this-world perspective.

A Roadmap for Life

How do you prefer to take vacations? Do you plan every moment, book the hotel, and make reservations at that one restaurant you've been dying to try, or do you simply get in the car and decide your destination as you go? Most people prefer to choose a route and outline an itinerary ahead of time. This takes away the anxiety of wondering if you'll find a vacant hotel and ensures you will see the sights you desire. Wouldn't it be nice to be given a road map or itinerary for life—one that not only shows our destination, but highlights scenic routes and stops along the way? The Bible serves as a guide for finding the road laid out for us. Trusting God's Word helps smooth out many of the potholes, while at the same time highlighting important sights no one should miss. We never need to feel lost again!

Jesus did not come and die just to help us select where we worship on Sundays or to offer us a ticket to heaven. He came for so much more. In Jesus, we are afforded the opportunity to put Him first in every area of our lives.

Who has more wisdom to share concerning how to conduct our business affairs, love our spouses, raise our kids, and contribute to our communities? Jesus was never meant to occupy only the religious slice of our lives—He came to be Lord of it all! With Jesus in the center of all aspects of life, we experience purpose and fulfillment throughout each day.

The second part of the Greatest Commandment involves loving our neighbor. Imagine how different the world would be if everyone treated others as more important than themselves. What would it look like to be committed to the thriving of our neighbor, even at our own expense? What if nations sought the betterment of each other rather than warring over land and resources?

In America, we honor charitable giving even to the point of offering a tax deduction for such gifts. The tithes and offerings of good people have fed those who are hungry and have built churches, hospitals, homeless shelters, and recreation centers. We love our neighbor by concerning ourselves enough with their pain to join them there, however we are able. David King, assistant professor of Philanthropic Studies at Indiana University–Purdue University Indianapolis (IUPUI), notes that, "With the majority of global citizens belonging to a religious tradition, it should be no surprise that religion often becomes the greatest asset in humanitarian work."[8]

Think back to a time when you did a kind deed for someone. How did that make you feel? Why does it warm our hearts to meet a need in another person, even if they are a perfect stranger? The apostle Paul sheds light on why when he says, "Do nothing from selfish ambition or conceit, but in humility count others more significant than yourselves. Let each of you look not only to his own interests, but also to the interests of others" (Phil. 2:3–4 ESV).

His point is that we were built to find fulfillment—purpose—by treating others the way we would like to be treated. This is the Golden Rule (see Matt. 7:12). Here is how King David described this inner longing to do what God says: "I desire to do your will, my God; your law is within my heart" (Ps. 40:8). Do you sense that is true in you as well?

What if it's true that loving God and loving others is our highest calling? What if this is our most basic purpose? Is it just a coincidence these biblical directives make our hearts sing? And, since following what the Bible says about serving others feels so good, I wonder if the rest of what the Bible teaches might also be fulfilling. What if it is all true? I believe that it is, and that God's people reflect God's character in the world when they love Him and serve others.

Discuss and Reflect

1. What would you like the legacy of your life to be? In other words, for what would you most like to be honored at your funeral?

2. What do you think it means when Jesus says, "I am the light of the world. Whoever follows me will never walk in darkness, but will have the light of life" (John 8:12)? Have you ever experienced this kind of illumination?

3. When have you experienced consequences from trying to find your own way in life rather than listening to Jesus?

4. What do you believe is God's purpose for your life? How motivating is that purpose for you?

4

What Is Truth and Where Is It Found?

Webster defines truth as "conformity to fact or reality; exact accordance with that which is, or has been; or shall be."[9] We all determine which reality to believe, but the quest for truth motivates each of us. In a Table Talk conversation from Ligonier Ministries in 2010, Dr. Steven J. Lawson said, "In a word, truth is reality. It is how things actually are. Theologically, truth is that which is consistent with the mind, will, character, glory, and being of God."[10] If we adhere to this definition it takes the pressure off of having to define for ourselves what to believe.

If truth and right living (righteousness) are given to us from above, then our task is to learn it, then live it—not invent it! No wonder anxiety is rampant in our culture—we're trying to invent what is true, and that is an endeavor above our pay grade.

Truth Decay

As of 2021, nearly three quarters of Americans say there is no such thing as absolute truth—something that is true at all times and in all places. A new term is being thrown around to describe this condition: *truth decay*. Popularized by Jennifer Kavanaugh of the Rand Corporation, truth decay is a cultural condition in which the very idea of absolute, objective, and universal truth is considered implausible and held in open contempt. The increased volume of commentary on social media and in news outlets further negates the focus on truth and amplifies that of opinion.[11] The consequences of this trend are far-reaching.

Almost every culture the world over condemns premeditated murder as being wrong and punishable by law. Protecting life is something human beings innately know to be right and true. Why? Because there is a moral compass within us that points favorably to what is good, and negatively toward what is wrong. So, the next time someone claims all truth is subjective, ask them if it is okay for you to steal their car. When they ask why you think that would be okay, simply reply, "My truth says I am free to take what I want, regardless of how you feel about it." This oversimplified illustration points to the flaw in moral relativism—the belief that each person is free to define truth for themselves.

Writing for Focus on the Family, Lindy Keffer explains the important function of absolute truth: "If we have ultimate truth, it gives us both a way to explain the world around us and a basis for making decisions. Without it, we're just 6 billion organisms running around bumping into each other with no common vision to unite us. It's every person for them self. If there ceases to be a true story of where we came from and why we're here, then there's nothing that gives our lives meaning or purpose."[12]

There is a movement today among some Christian churches called *deconstructionism* that is predicated on the belief that we need to unravel our faith from the cultural parameters often set by God's people. Deconstruction looks different person to person, and while some remove their faith completely, others still believe God's Word is authoritative. They just believe their interpretation can be more informed by our unique perspectives instead of the historic beliefs of the church. Uncomfortable with certain aspects they see in "cultural Christianity," many seek to deconstruct their beliefs and practices, and reconstruct a faith based on an interpretation of the Scriptures that feels more relevant and consistent with their worldview.

Proponents of this practice affirm their quest for truth, while critics fear that deconstructionists reject the authority of the Holy Scriptures and only keep what feels good to them. We are cautioned by history to avoid a consistent human error where, "In those days there was no king in Israel; everyone did what was right in his own eyes" (Judg. 21:25 NASB1995). And they experienced God's wrath as a result of their disobedience to divinely revealed truth.

Truth is not a discovery of something new, but a continuation of something ancient. What is true should not be up for debate, but should be mined from the depths of history. Truth and how to enforce the morality surrounding it have been the backbone for societies since people began to live in villages with one another, guiding how their people live, act, and believe.

For the first 180 years of America, Judeo-Christian values were considered not only good for society, but also to be derived from two accepted sources of truth: the Bible and long-standing tradition. Our founding fathers established laws based on right and wrong prescribed in the Bible. Consider the consequences we as a society are frantically trying to navigate as a result of turning our backs on what God said is important for our mutual thriving: questions of identity, family values and the strength of the nuclear family, sexual ethics, and beyond. God has provided His Word so that we might know how humanity will most flourish, but often, we run in the opposite direction as a society.

Society as a whole, not just individuals, reaps the consequences of doing what is right in our own eyes, rather than obeying our source of a truth. But what if it's all true? How might we live if God's Word really is the standard for truth?

Why Does Truth Seem So Elusive?

Following Jesus's arrest, He eventually is turned over to the Roman governor Pontius Pilate. At one point in His questioning Jesus tells Pilate, "The reason I was born and came into the world is to testify to the truth. Everyone on the side of truth listens to me" (John 18:37). Pilate then famously replies, "What is truth?" (v. 38). This is a very relevant question for us today.

Our culture values pluralism, equity, and belonging (all good things!), so declaring something as absolutely true comes with the fear that we might offend a person or group. Many are so offense-adverse that they would find it difficult to consider promoting one belief above others, even if they are convinced that belief is absolute. Yet, we, as Christians, hold the words of life! Jesus said, "I am the way, the truth, and the life. No one comes to the Father except through me" (John 14:6 CSB). Either this statement is completely true or completely false—there is no ambiguity.

The law of non-contradiction, first purported by Aristotle, states that, if one statement is true, its opposite statement cannot also be true in the same respect at the same time. For example, Jesus cannot be both sinless and sinful, or finite and also infinite. He must be one or the other. Human beings cannot be the result of nontheistic evolution and also the result of an intentional Creator. Only one can be true. You get the point.

What Is the Source of Absolute Truth?

Psalm 19:7–9 (CSB) says:

> The instruction of the LORD is perfect, renewing one's life; the testimony of the LORD is trustworthy, making the inexperienced wise. The precepts of the LORD are right, making the heart glad; the command of the LORD is radiant, making the eyes light up. The fear of the LORD is pure, enduring forever; the ordinances of the LORD are reliable and altogether righteous.

How does this testimony of Scripture align with your view?

The Bible does not present truth as a cultural creation of the ancient Jews or early Christians. They recorded truth directly received from the God who speaks truth to His creatures, and they were expected to conform their lives to this truth. Why wouldn't they, if they trusted the source?

Knowing what we believe and why will serve as a foundation for nearly everything we say and do. If culture, our feelings, or the hottest trends are what drive our worldview, we won't only misjudge small matters—we will get everything wrong!

Conclusion

Western culture today would like us to think how we feel about something determines its validity, that feelings alone can determine truth. Of course, we have feelings, often passionate feelings, about what is going on around us. But the key questions to ask are: What is the bedrock that informs our feelings? Can we reliably demonstrate that our feelings align with God's unchanging Word? If we do not stand on the authority of the One who said, "I am the truth" (John 14:6), what will we stand on? Is it not the epitome of arrogance to think we have the fullness of knowledge to decide all truth for ourselves?

Tim Keller makes the case that "Christians seek spiritual renewal of the church not because they see religion as having social utility, nor because they want to shore up their own institutions.

Rather, we believe Christianity is relevant to society because it's true."[13]

May the Lord keep us mindful that there's only one Truth. It's been revealed in the person of Jesus and in His authoritative Word. This Truth is reliable, unchanging, and invulnerable to the cultural sand shifting beneath our feet.

Discuss and Reflect

1. Do you believe in absolute truth? Why or why not?

2. Is your standard for what is true based on how you feel on a given day, or is it based on some universal truth you accept?

3. Do you think God's directives in the Bible limit our fulfillment or offer a pathway to it?

5

Where Do We Get Clarity about God?

Ilana Horwitz wrote in the *New York Times* in March 2022, "Many in the American intelligentsia—the elite-university-educated population who constitute the professional and managerial class—do not hold the institution of religion in high regard. When these elites criticize religion, they often do so on the grounds that faith (in their eyes) is irrational and not evidence-based."[14] You may agree or disagree with Ms. Horwitz's thoughts, but I would like to devote this chapter to countering the assertion that the Christian faith is not founded on sound evidence. The source that for two millennia the masses have trusted, God's Word, was written down by the hands of eyewitnesses to reveal His truth to all generations.

As John wrote at the end of his Gospel, "Jesus performed many other signs in the presence of his disciples, which are not recorded in this book. But these are written that you may believe that Jesus is the Messiah, the Son of God, and that by believing you may have life in his name" (John 20:30–32).

Quite often people with minimal knowledge of the Bible say things like, "That's just your interpretation," implying the Bible is intentionally vague and open to our own deciphering. Yes, some passages are open for scholarly interpretation that land in slightly different places, but the Bible is not a broadly subjective literary source open to our own commentary. The field of study for interpretation, called hermeneutics, lays out a detailed series of steps, practices, disciplines, and rules that guide scriptural interpretation. Wise reading of Scripture seeks to follow wise practices toward doing so like reading within the passage's context, both historical and literary; allowing Scripture to interpret Scripture; and observing and interpreting before seeking to apply a text.

The good news is that 99 percent of the Bible doesn't demand seminary-trained insight to understand its meaning because a plain reading of the text gives us all we need to know. Author and cultural commentator James Emery White offers the following:

> In the Old Testament book of Deuteronomy it says, "Hear, O Israel: The Lord our God, the Lord is one." So, is there one God or two? One! In the Old Testament book of Exodus it says, "You shall not steal." Is it okay to steal or not? It's not! In the New Testament book of 1 Thessalonians it says, "Jesus died and rose again" (4:14). Did Jesus die and rise again or not? The Bible says that He did.[15]

So is the Bible really all that obscure in its meaning? I don't think so!

Overview on the Reliability of Scripture

There is great evidence to support the reliability of the Scriptures. In this section, we will briefly explore four major pieces of evidence that substantiate the reliability of the Bible as a trusted source of truth.

1. Bibliographic Evidence

The bibliographic evidence examines the transmission of the text of the Old and New Testaments from the original writings to present day.

There are more New Testament manuscripts than Old Testament. However, the Hebrew manuscripts have incredible reliability due to the meticulous protocols governing the Hebrew scribes who recorded them. Any manuscript with even one error was destroyed, so while there are fewer manuscripts, we can assume their credibility due to the lack of discrepancies among the copies we do have.

The quantity of New Testament manuscripts far surpasses any other document in ancient literature. We have more than fourteen thousand copies of New Testament manuscripts plus tens of thousands of citations of New Testament passages by the early church fathers. Our modern New Testaments can be regarded as 99.5 percent accurate. The remaining 0.5 percent can be ascertained with a high degree of probability by the practice of textual criticism that examines the evidence about written works in an attempt to recover the original text.[16] None of these discrepancies among manuscripts affect key theological concepts, so even where there are differences, the thrust of the argument within Scripture is unaffected by them.

The chart[17] on the next page shows a comparison of New Testament manuscripts with other ancient writings.

2. External Evidence

The Bible constantly refers to historical events that are verifiable. Their accuracy can be checked by external evidence. The historicity of Jesus Christ is well-established by early Roman, Greek, and Jewish sources. One of the most famous recorders of Jesus within history was named Flavius Josephus. Josephus refers to Jesus as a teacher and leader. He also refers to Pilate and his dealings with Jesus and to John the Baptist. So these key biblical characters are referenced in other ancient documents, further substantiating their significance in the Bible.[18]

Archeological evidence, though incomplete at this point, continues to provide external confirmation of hundreds of biblical statements. Archeology has played a critical role in giving the Bible a strong reputation for its historical accuracy. To date, there has been no major archeological find that directly refutes any claim in the Bible. Instead, the thousands of finds only serve to further validate the scriptural accounts.

Author	Date Written	Earliest Copy	Time Span	Number of Copies	Accuracy
Homer	ca. 850 B.C.	-------------	-------------	643	95%
Herodotus	ca. 450 B.C.	ca. A.D. 900	About 1,350 years	8	Not enough copies to reconstruct the original
Euripedes	ca. 440 B.C.	ca. A.D. 1100	About 1,500 years	9	
Thucydides	ca. 420 B.C.	ca. A.D. 900	About 1,300 years	8	
Plato	ca. 380 B.C.	ca. A.D. 900	About 1,300 years	7	
Aristotle	ca. 350 B.C.	ca. A.D. 1100	About 1,400 years	5	
Caesar	ca. 60 B.C.	ca. A.D. 900	About 950 years	10	
Catullus	ca. 50 B.C.	ca. A.D. 1500	About 1,600 years	3	
Livy	ca. 10 B.C.	-------------	-------------	20	
Tacitus	ca. A.D. 100	ca. A.D. 1100	About 1,000 years	20	
New Testament	ca. A.D. 60	ca. A.D. 130	About 100 years	14,000	99.5%

3. Internal Evidence

The bulk of the Bible was written by men who were eye-witnesses of the events they recorded. The Gospels were written during a time when some eyewitnesses were still living, and many who heard the testimony of eyewitnesses firsthand were the ones helping tell the story. If there were any blatant historical fabrications, then the books and letters would have been challenged by the people at that time. They were not. It also makes a strong case for reliability that the apostles were martyred for their belief in what the Scriptures teach as truth. Who would die to perpetuate a lie?

Inventing the Scriptures would have been a miracle in itself. There is too much unity for the writers to have successfully forged it since the Bible was written by forty authors, over a period of fifteen hundred years, in three different languages, on three different continents, in an era without phone lines or Internet. The New Testament quotes the Old Testament over six hundred times. The Bible has literally thousands of verifiable historical prophecies, cases in which events were clearly foretold, and both the foretelling and the fulfillment are a matter of historical record. It would be too difficult to invent the sayings and miracles of Jesus and have them correspond perfectly with Old Testament prophecy. The evidence from the Scriptures themselves is enough to prove its validity.

4. The Testimony of Faith

Trusting the Bible to be the inspired Word of God comes through faith—not blind faith, but informed faith. Yes, there are many important evidences outside of faith to confirm its validity, but to believe that God was the ultimate author is a matter of trust. Millions of people over the centuries have given testimony to the life change God has worked in them through His Word, and these continue today.

In closing, the Bible tells us we are not mistakes, but rather the beautiful creation of a personal God who not only loves each one of us, but has a purpose and plan for our lives that is found only in a committed, personal relationship with Him. If we trust this well-substantiated source of inspiration, then the promises throughout the Bible are true for us who lean into them, and we join those who have held this testimony of faith throughout the centuries. Let's keep leaning in!

> "For I know the plans I have for you," declares the LORD, "plans to prosper you and not to harm you, plans to give you hope and a future." (Jer. 29:11)

What if it's all true?

Discuss and Reflect

1. Before reading this chapter, what did you believe about the accuracy of the Bible?

2. Did anything you read in this chapter alter how you view the Scriptures?

3. If the Bible is what it claims to be, the inspired infallible Word of God, how should you responsibly handle it going forward?

6

What Is Right and Wrong?

Are there things out there that bother you, that make you exclaim, "That isn't right!" I had this reaction as I saw harrowing images on television of Ukrainian women and children being bombed by the Russians on an evacuation route during a supposed cease-fire.

To judge this as wrong means there is a standard by which we determine right from wrong. Is your standard based on how you feel on a given day or by what seems to be culturally trending? Or is what you consider right and wrong consistently woven into your character and known to be true regardless of external influences? It is no mistake that nearly every country considers murder, stealing, and lying to be wrong and punishable in a court of law. The existence of such widely accepted standards points to a consistent sense of truth inside of us. Where does this sense come from? Is it by accident or by design?

Recently I heard a report about a middle school teacher who decided he was identifying as a woman one particular day, so he took a nude sauna in the girls' locker room. Shocked teen girls ran to another teacher to report the horrific scene. Their teacher rebuked and reported the male to their principal. However, she, not the man, was disciplined for being intolerant. Does this really make sense to rational people? Chaos is the final result of the rejection of absolute truth, and it is rearing its ugly head a lot these days!

Other examples flood the daily news: smash-and-grab bandits making off with thousands of dollars' worth of merchandise but not being prosecuted, or elderly people being beaten to a pulp by a robber only interested in stealing the few bucks in their purse. These images haunt us for a reason. But there are loads of positive images that also serve as confirmation that we are hardwired with a standard for right and wrong.

We honor as heroes those who sacrifice their lives for the sake of others—even people they do not know. We honor our military men and women and first responders who stand ready at a moment's notice to jump into harm's way for our sake. The news cycles also honor good Samaritans like one I read about today who stepped into a fight in a restaurant to disarm a knife-wielding man attacking a waitress. He did what was right despite great risk to himself, and we recognize the attacker for doing what we know is wrong.

Logically, we cannot know something is "wrong" unless some things are known deep within us to be "right." How do we know what is right? Did humility, mercy, or sensitivity to others develop via evolution? They certainly are not required for the survival of the fittest. The Bible tells us these characteristics were imbedded in our DNA by our Creator who created man like Himself, "in his own image" (Gen. 1:27). That means that, unlike anything else in the created order, God imbued man with the ability to think and reason, to determine right from wrong. If this is true, then why do some people view injustices similar to those just described through a different lens? Which view is accurate?

The Bible tells us that God made us with a free will. He did not want us to be robots forced to follow Him. No! He desired that we follow Him because He is loving and just. The Israelites responded to the Law because they knew it was life-giving, not burdensome. They sought flourishing and knew God's commands were the fence around the field to lead them to this desired outcome.

But when the very first humans decided to disobey God, sin entered the world and His perfect creation was now corrupted (see Genesis 3 for context). Here is one explanation for why so many people view right and wrong differently: "Satan, who is the god of this world, has blinded the minds of those who don't believe. They are unable to see the glorious light of the Good News. They don't understand this message about the glory of Christ, who is the exact likeness of God" (2 Cor. 4:4 NLT).

Our economy depends on the production and protection of property and goods, so we know deep down that stealing is wrong. I wonder if we know that because one of the Ten Commandments (better translated "Ten Wise Ideas for a Flourishing Life") says,

"Do not steal" (Exod. 20:15 csb)? If stealing were to be left unchecked and followed to its logical conclusion, imagine how chaotic society would be.

Today's news shows Florida declaring a state of emergency in Miami due to the out-of-control revelers there for spring break. Violence, shootings, and intoxicated people are acting out in destructive ways. Gee, I wonder why God's Word says to not murder (Exod. 20:13) and to be of sound mind rather than intoxicated (1 Pet. 1:13; Eph. 5:18). Did God command this because He is mean and doesn't want us to have fun? Or is it to help us experience the full life He intends unencumbered by worldly vices? Might God's commands actually be good news?

Let's look at one more of the Wise Ideas for a Flourishing Life. How is your work/life balance? (Something I have sure struggled with!) Anxiety is rampant in this country, as are mental breakdowns. Suicides are heartbreakingly on the rise. This causes me to wonder if a Sabbath day of rest to remind us what matters most could be a key to a healthier rhythm of life. Chick-fil-A has been criticized for closing on Sundays, yet their business is flourishing and their employees are unusually positive. Might there be application here for us personally?

If it's true what God says is right and good, why do we resist it? The quest for independence is what led to original sin, and it still motivates us to sin today. It is why teenagers often rebel against their parents' authority. We value deciding for ourselves how to live, rather than being under the authority of another. This has been a mark of the human condition since the beginning of time—they "did what was right in [their] own eyes" (Judg. 17:6 ESV), which as we saw above in 2 Corinthians 4:3–4, is exactly what the Evil One desires.

Our penchant for independence seeks to convince us otherwise, but when we experience the fulfillment these godly directives bring, we get a taste of righteousness, which means things working according to their intended purpose. Righteousness is experienced when we say yes to God and no to ourselves. Righteous deeds feel good because they are morally right and just, thus freeing us from guilt or shame.

When a complex plumbing system is free from clogs or kinks in the pipes, it is considered a righteous system. Water flows freely without encumbrance. It flourishes! Similarly, when we submit to God and live as He asks us to, we experience righteousness, bringing a level of satisfaction to our souls. As Solomon, the wisest man who ever lived, wrote, "Adversity pursues sinners, But the righteous will be rewarded . . ." (Prov. 13:21 NASB1995).

In college, most of my friends were experimenting with drugs and having sex with their girlfriends or boyfriends. I chose to say yes in faith to what God says is best and no to these trends. I remained part of the in-crowd and, rather than losing friends over this, I actually gained their respect. I observed the pain of their guilt after a one-night stand, and I'm thankful I didn't have to operate in that shame and was able to give my wife my virginity on our wedding night. Our yes to God allows us to experience the deep, lasting life He desires for us. This is righteousness.

What qualities do you look for in a friend? Selfish, temperamental, arrogant, lazy, stingy? Of course not! We want friends who are loving, kind, generous, and forgiving. How is it possible that nearly everyone the world over embraces these same positive virtues if we are all free to decide morality for ourselves? The Bible says these qualities are imbued in us by our Creator: "Put on then . . . compassionate hearts, kindness, humility, meekness, and patience, bearing with one another and, if one has a complaint against another, forgiving each other; as the Lord has forgiven you, so you also must forgive" (Col. 3:12–13 ESV).

As we put into practice what the Bible teaches, we grow in these God-modeled, God-inspired characteristics that yield righteous living. And we grow to believe more and more in God's ultimate truth! What if it's all true?

Discuss and Reflect

1. What has caused you to exclaim, "That isn't right!"? How did you come to that conclusion?

2. Upon what source, or sources, do you rely for truth?

3. What words describe your view of God's commands for how He intends us to live?

4. Is there an area of your life you would like to trust God with and follow what He says?

Has the World Been
Intelligently Designed?

During my undergraduate experience I took a number of courses in the Earth Sciences department. I found the study of Earth—its origins, topography, and ecosystems—fascinating. One of my geology professors, whom I will refer to as "Dr. B," was an absolutely brilliant man who could lecture from textbooks written in Russian, German, or English. He taught the Historical Geology course that included the origin of the universe, Earth, and all of life. Dr. B did his best to convince us that Earth is about six billion years old and that all life evolved by chance from nothing. Even though Dr. B's brilliance made me want to buy into his theory of evolution, I couldn't muster the faith required as it was too full of holes and lacked scientific evidence.

It makes much more sense to me that we are the result of an intentional Creator who took the time to make lakes, mountains,

islands, and all the rest a blessing to behold. And as the epitome
of His handiwork, the Creator made human beings, you and me,
in His image. We are a wonder and statistical miracle to behold!

I encourage you to examine this chapter with an open mind
to see what appeals to your sense of rationality. I think you'll be
glad you did!

One of the laws employed in the field of logic is the law of
rationality, which states that one should accept as true only those
conclusions for which there is adequate evidence. This is sensible,
for accepting a conclusion as true without evidence, or with inad-
equate evidence, would not only be irrational, but potentially
harmful. When we look at design in the universe through the
lens of rationality, what conclusions might we draw regarding the
origin of life?

Design in Nature—The Teleological Argument

This approach suggests that where there is purposeful design,
there must be a designer. You wouldn't come upon a beautiful
home and wonder if it built itself without an architect or crafts-
men, would you? No. Order, planning, design, and competence
are obvious in the structure, engineering, and complexity of the
building. A theist is someone who believes in a Creator God who
has inserted Himself in the created order. They would say the
universe shows clear, purposeful design; therefore, it is the work of
an intentional designer.

Design in the Universe

Our universe operates in accordance with scientific laws. The precision of the universe allows scientists to launch rockets to the moon with the full knowledge that, upon their arrival, they can land within a few feet of their intended target. It's phenomenal, and only possible through the design and certainty found in these laws. Consider these fun facts to know and tell:

- The earth is rotating on its axis at 1,000 miles per hour at the equator and moving around the sun at a speed of 19 miles per second.[19] (As a guy who likes to race cars, this kind of speed gets my adrenaline flowing!) The sun and its solar system are moving through space at 600,000 miles per hour in an orbit so large it would take more than 220 million years just to complete a single lap. Interestingly, though, as the earth moves in its orbit around the sun, it departs from a straight line by only one-ninth of an inch every eighteen miles.[20] If it departed by one-eighth of an inch, we would come so close to the sun that we would be incinerated. If it departed by one-tenth of an inch, we would find ourselves so far from the sun that we would all freeze to death.[21]

- The earth is positioned some 240,000 miles from the moon, whose gravitational pull produces the oceans' tides. If the moon were closer to the earth by just a fifth, the tides would be so enormous that twice a day they would reach nearly fifty feet high over most of the earth's surface.[22]

- The oceans provide a vast reservoir of moisture that is constantly evaporating and condensing, thus falling upon the land as rain. Since water holds its temperature longer than land masses, it provides a natural heating and air-conditioning system for the land across the earth. Temperature extremes would be much more erratic were it not for the fact that approximately four-fifths of the earth is covered with water. In addition, humans and animals inhale oxygen and exhale carbon dioxide. Plants take in carbon dioxide and give off oxygen. We depend on the world of botany for our oxygen supply, but often fail to realize that approximately 90 percent of our oxygen comes from microscopic plants in the seas. If our oceans were smaller, we soon would be out of air to breathe.[23]

Can a person reasonably be expected to believe that these requirements for life as we know it have been met merely by chance?

The earth:

- is exactly the right distance from the sun.
- is exactly the right distance from the moon.
- is exactly the right diameter.
- is exactly the right atmospheric pressure.
- has exactly the right tilt.
- has exactly the right amount of oceanic water.
- has exactly the right weight and mass.

And so on.

Were these many requirements to be met in any other essential area of life, the idea that they had been provided by accident would quickly be dismissed as impossible.

Even atheist Richard Dawkins admits, "The more statistically improbable a thing is, the less we can believe that it just happened by blind chance. Superficially, the obvious alternative to chance is an intelligent Designer."[24] Theists have drawn this same conclusion from the available evidence corresponding with the law of rationality. The statistical improbability of the universe "just happening by blind chance" is staggering. The only alternative is an intelligent Designer. Consider the possibilities if it's all true.

Design of the Human Body

To secular humanists our bodies are merely the result of fortu-
itous circumstances credited to the natural outworking of nature.
Yet such a suggestion moves even staunch evolutionists to agree
with the late George Gaylord Simpson of Harvard, who suggested
that, in man one finds "the most highly endowed organization of
matter that has yet appeared on the earth . . ."[25] If this is true, a
divine Designer certainly must be involved.

Take the nucleus of a cell: the nucleus is the control center
of the cell and is separated from the cytoplasm by a nuclear
membrane. Within the nucleus is the genetic machinery of the
cell (chromosomes and genes containing deoxyribonucleic acid—
DNA). The DNA is a super molecule that carries the coded
information for the replication of the cell. If the DNA from a
single human cell were removed from the nucleus and unraveled,
it would be approximately six feet long and would contain over a
billion biochemical steps. It has been estimated that if all the DNA
in an adult human were placed end-to-end, it would reach to the
sun and back (186 million miles) four hundred times.[26]

It should also be noted that the DNA molecule does something we humans have yet to accomplish: it stores coded information in a chemical format and then uses a biologic agent (RNA) to
decode and activate it.

The complexity and intricacy of the DNA molecule—com-
bined with the staggering amount of chemically coded information
it contains—speak unerringly to the fact that this supermolecule

simply could not have happened by blind chance. As physicist Edgar Andrews observed: "It is not possible for a code, of any kind, to arise by chance or accident. . . . A code is the work of an intelligent mind. This could no more have been the work of chance than could the 'Moonlight Sonata' be played by mice running up and down the keyboard of my piano! Codes do not arise from chaos."[27]

Can one reasonably be expected to conclude that the structural masterpiece of the human body—with its ingenious systems and highly endowed organization—is the result of blind chance operating over eons of time in nature as atheism suggests? Or would it be more in keeping with the facts to suggest that the human body is the result of purposeful design by a Master Designer? If so, do you suppose that Designer, like any good parent, would want to be involved with His masterpiece throughout their life?

Conclusion

There is a spiritual answer as to why even seemingly smart people have difficulty assigning the phenomenal order and of the universe to a Creator God: "The natural person does not accept the things of the Spirit of God, for they are folly to him, and he is not able to understand them because they are spiritually discerned" (1 Cor. 2:14 ESV). However, the evidence is clear. God has intricately designed the universe and is sustaining it. One does not get a poem without a poet, or a law without a lawgiver. And just as surely, one does not get purposeful design without a designer.[28]

What if it's all true?

Discuss and Reflect

1. What facts of the intricacy of the creation most cause you to marvel?

2. Do you believe the exacting requirements for life on planet Earth have been met merely by chance, or do they demand a Creator behind them?

3. If there is a Creator behind your life, how interested do you think He is in seeing you through every step of the way? How interested are you in Him?

8

What Do You See When You
Look in the Mirror?

When I was eight, my parents began designing their dream house. They poured themselves into every detail. During construction, we would drive out to see the progress each weekend. My folks wanted to ensure every nook and cranny was built to specs, and they couldn't wait to move into their masterpiece. We lived in that house for sixteen wonderful years. My parents, now quite elderly, still enjoy driving past to admire their workmanship. One of the few things my dad (who struggles with dementia) still recalls is their choice of brick: "Calvert Rose with darks deleted."

If we are the handiwork of an intentional Creator, who has even numbered the hairs on our heads (Matt. 10:30), do you think He would create us and then move on to the next, more important task without seeing us through? Or, would He more likely want to be intimately involved with the fruit of His labor? Even we imperfect parents desire to walk with our kids through each chapter of life. How much more so does our perfect heavenly Father?

God is not a watchmaker who made the world, stepped back, and let it tick to its logical end. Instead, He is intimately involved in His creation, near to His work. And because He has created all things, He has authority over all things and He knows how His creation works best. This means He has authority to instruct His creation and to impose structures for purity, healthy living, and loving relationships.

Scripture consistently communicates that this personal Creator desires to walk hand in hand with us throughout each day. He wants to be in the center of every aspect of our lives—social, work, family, hobbies, all of it—and this is for our good, because God is good. All He does is right:

- "I give them eternal life, and they will never perish. . . . No one can snatch them from the Father's hand." (John 10:28–29 NLT)
- "The LORD, in whose presence I have lived, will send his angel with you and will make your mission successful." (Gen. 24:40a NLT)
- ". . . the LORD has told you what is good, and this is what he requires of you: to do what is right, to love mercy, and to walk humbly with your God." (Micah 6:8 NLT)
- "For you created my inmost being; you knit me together in my mother's womb. I praise

you because I am fearfully and wonderfully
made." (Ps. 139:13–14a)

Solomon wisely said, God has "set eternity in the human
heart" (Eccles. 3:11). No wonder every civilization discovered has
been found to have worshipped some sort of deity. Humanity
innately senses that there is a Creator behind this thing called
life—a Creator we long to worship, know, and understand.
Imagine the peace available to those who are convinced that life is
in the control of a loving God. What assurance this brings!

Why is it that so many fail to connect with this intimate,
personal side of God? Scripture consistently tells us that those who
walk in darkness (apart from the Lord) have spiritual blinders on
their eyes. They cannot see the truth. The apostle Paul addressed
this tendency to the ancient peoples of Corinth: "But their minds
were hardened. For to this day, when they read the old covenant,
that same veil remains unlifted, because only through Christ is
it taken away. . . . But when one turns to the Lord, the veil is
removed" (2 Cor. 3:14, 16 ESV). The Old Testament prophet,
Isaiah, similarly noted, "They know nothing, they understand
nothing; their eyes are plastered over so they cannot see, and their
minds closed so they cannot understand" (Isa. 44:18).

"Their eyes are plastered over." What a description! This
blindness is the defining factor of the one who does not trust God.
Following Jesus's resurrection, a few of His followers were walking
along the road from Jerusalem to Emmaus when a stranger joined
them. ". . . while they conversed and reasoned, . . . Jesus Himself
drew near and went with them. But their eyes were restrained, so

that they did not know Him" (Luke 24:15–16 NKJV). Then Jesus opened the Scriptures for them and broke bread, and their eyes were opened. When they could see clearly, they recognized and worshipped Jesus as their Creator and Lord.

"If the Good News we preach is hidden behind a veil, it is hidden only from people who are perishing. Satan, who is the god of this world, has blinded the minds of those who don't believe. They are unable to see the glorious light of the Good News. They don't understand this message about the glory of Christ, who is the exact likeness of God" (2 Cor. 4:3–4 NLT). We need the Light of the world to show us the way to abundant life, and the way to recognize and see Him clearly is to ask the Spirit to remove the blinders from our eyes to see the intentional handiwork of God in creation. He spoke every element into existence, with more care than the most diligent of couples building their home together. He has built up His world and told us how it works best in His Word. We can trust what He says is true about how He has created us.

Discuss and Reflect

1. Do you believe God desires to be a part of every piece of your life, or just the religious slice?

2. How might we go about inviting Him into the center of every part of our lives?

3. Do you think it is true that "Satan, who is the god of this world, has blinded the minds of those who don't believe. They are unable to see the glorious light of the Good News. They don't understand this message about the glory of Christ, who is the exact likeness of God" (2 Cor. 4:4 NLT)? If so, what can be done to remove the blinders?

9

Who Is Jesus?

In a world where we're inundated with information and opinions abound, the question "Who is Jesus of Nazareth?" stands as foundational above all others. How we answer this question informs every area of our life. It influences our character, who we marry, how we raise our children, our goals, and ultimately, our eternal destiny. We operate out of a sense of the answer to this question, even if we do not believe and we have not considered it carefully. With stakes this high, it is worth determining who you believe Jesus to be, just as Peter did in what we call the Christological confession in Mark 8:27–30.

Muslims believe Jesus was a wise prophet, Hindus believe He was an avatar, modern Jews believe He was a great teacher, but all agree no one has impacted mankind more than Jesus of Nazareth. Yale historian Jaroslav Pelikan wrote, "Regardless of what anyone may personally believe about him, Jesus of Nazareth has been the dominant figure in the history of Western Culture for almost 20 centuries."[29]

What did those who knew Jesus personally conclude about His identity? "Philip found Nathanael and told him, 'We have found the one Moses wrote about in the Law, and about whom the prophets also wrote—Jesus of Nazareth, the son of Joseph'" (John 1:45). For hundreds of years before His birth, prophecies describing the person and mission of Jesus had consistently been passed along, both in writing and by oral tradition. The Jews understood that God was going to send His Son to be the Messiah, the one who would redeem Israel. No wonder these early disciples were thrilled to encounter the Son of Man, God taking on flesh, so all of mankind might understand and know Him in a personal way.

What Was the Incarnation?

John 1:14 (PHILLIPS) describes what we call the Incarnation. It reads: "The word of God [Jesus] became a human being and lived among us." God chose to become a man so we might not only know of Him from a distance but could know Him personally. The Incarnation allows us to see God's character fleshed out in a human being. Jesus was born of an earthly mother but was conceived by the Holy Spirit (Matt. 1:18). He felt pain, temptation, suffering, compassion, and great loss. He sought to identify with the human experience.

There is a beautiful example of the personalness of God shown by Jesus in John 11. Jesus weeps with His dear friends Mary and Martha over the apparent death of their brother, Lazarus, who was also a close companion of Jesus. How comforting it is to know that Jesus weeps with us when we are downtrodden, the same way He celebrates with us when we are elated.

Jesus shows how God empathizes with our life experiences because He not only lived them, He overcame them. Thanks to Jesus, our Creator no longer needs to seem distant or something to fear. He shows incredible compassion and love for His people. Jesus's prayer in the garden of Gethsemane the night before He was crucified perfectly reveals how deeply God loves you and me today. He says He is not just praying for the disciples with Him then, but "also for those who will believe in me through their message . . . Then the world will know that you sent me and have loved them even as you have loved me" (John 17:20, 23b). Wow! What if it's true that God loves you to the same extent He loved His only Son, Jesus? What response does that provoke?

Prior to the Incarnation, God's people had experienced God most often through judgment and correction. They had seen mighty acts of deliverance and providence, but there was also separation because of man's sin. Moses spoke directly with God as a priest who mediated for the people, but God was not easily accessible for the everyday person. This led to many misconceptions about Him. By becoming a human being, we are blessed to see God with skin on. Our vision of Him is now tangible. And because Jesus lived a sin-free and perfect life, He, unlike any other, was able to pay the penalty for our sin so we could be forgiven and have direct access to God. Read below a few Scriptures that describe the Incarnation of Jesus:

- "But when the fullness of time had come, God sent forth his Son, born of woman, born under the law, to redeem those who were under the law, so that we might receive adoption as sons." (Gal. 4:4–5 ESV)

- "Now Christ is the visible expression of the invisible God." (Col. 1:15 PHILLIPS)

- "Because he himself [Jesus] suffered when he was tempted, he is able to help those who are being tempted." (Heb. 2:18)

- "Long ago, at many times and in many ways, God spoke to our fathers by the prophets, but in these last days he has spoken to us by his Son, whom he appointed the heir of all things, through whom also he created the world." (Heb. 1:1–2 ESV)

- "And being found in human form, he [Jesus] humbled himself by becoming obedient to the point of death, even death on a cross." (Phil. 2:8 ESV)

- "For Christ also suffered once for sins, the righteous for the unrighteous, to bring you to God. He was put to death in the body but made alive in the Spirit." (1 Pet. 3:18)

Consider for a moment these indelible marks Jesus has made on culture:

- In the ancient world children were routinely left to die of exposure—particularly if they were not the more desired gender. The priority Jesus showed to children brought an end to this practice and inspired the formation of orphanages.

- Jesus's compassion for the poor and lame was the inspiration for hospitals and mental facilities. It is no surprise that many hospitals today are named after a saint or biblical figure.

- People in ancient times were usually divided by class—the wealthy interacting with the wealthy, and poor with other poor. Humility was not a sought-after virtue as much as was bravery and wisdom. Jesus showed humility by washing the feet of those who saw themselves as beneath Him. His substitutionary atonement for our sin is not only the ultimate act of love, but of humility as well.

- Perhaps the most culturally radical example embodied by Jesus was His inclusion of women in His community. While the twelve disciples were all men, there were many women in the larger group of followers. This mixed-sex

> fraternity of friends became an example for
> future cultures to adopt. The apostle Paul said,
> "There is no longer Jew or Gentile, slave or
> free, male and female. For you are all one in
> Christ Jesus" (Gal. 3:28 NLT).

Who was Jesus? Those who knew Him best were pressed to answer this question following a very difficult teaching Jesus delivered in John chapter 6. Because they misinterpreted what Jesus was teaching, many of His followers left Him. So, Jesus turned to His twelve disciples and asked, "Do you want to go away as well?" (John 6:67 ESV). Simon Peter answered on behalf of the group: "Lord, to whom shall we go? You have the words of eternal life, and we have believed, and have come to know, that you are the Holy One of God" (vv. 68–69 ESV).

Every person who has ever lived is a believer in something or someone. I suggest there is no more credible person in all of history in whom to place a confident belief than Jesus of Nazareth. C. S. Lewis taught that an honest reflection on Jesus can only lead to one of three conclusions. He was either a liar—someone who made wild claims for His own ends—or He was a lunatic who actually believed He was God's Son but of course was not. The only other conclusion is that Jesus is Lord.[30] He simply cannot be reduced, as other world religions do, to a nice guy or wise teacher.

The apostle Paul modeled an understanding of the truth about who Jesus is with full-hearted devotion to Him, declaring, "For to me, to live is Christ and to die is gain" (Phil. 1:21). This devotion cost Paul significantly, but the truth was more valuable than his comfort or security; it was more valuable than his life to him. He said,

> I have . . . been in prison more frequently, been flogged more severely, and been exposed to death again and again. Five times I received from the Jews the forty lashes minus one. Three times I was beaten with rods, once I was pelted with stones, three times I was shipwrecked, I spent a night and a day in the open sea, I have been constantly on the move. I have been in danger from rivers, in danger from bandits, in danger from my fellow Jews, in danger from Gentiles; in danger in the city, in danger in the country, in danger at sea; and in danger from false believers. I have labored and toiled and have often gone without sleep; I have known hunger and thirst and have often gone without food; I have been cold and naked. (2 Cor. 11:23b–27)

One would never describe Paul's relationship with Jesus as being only "moderately significant." Jesus was his all in all, and he wouldn't have traded it for all the money in the world!

What if this sort of inspired devotion is available to you and me today? What if it's all true?

Discuss and Reflect

1. How would you describe the Incarnation? Why was it important for God to take on human form?

2. What qualities of God demonstrated by Jesus do you find the most attractive?

3. C. S. Lewis taught that an honest reflection on Jesus can only lead to one of three conclusions: He was a liar, a lunatic, or Lord. How do you conclude, and what are the implications of your belief for the rest of your life?

10

What Has Jesus Promised His Followers?

Have you ever felt like God put something in your path just to bring you a little joy? To remind you that you are seen and loved by Him? Once when climbing in the Wind River Mountains of Wyoming, I was ascending a fourteen-thousand-foot peak when I reached up for a handhold and found a beautiful purple flower growing out of a crag in the rocks. Obviously, the wind had blown a seed there and erosion had provided the minimum amount of dirt required for it to grow. I may have been the only person who would ever see that flower since it was not on a regular route. I surmised the Lord had put it there just for me!

It strikes me how much our Creator loves to shower us with beauty and blessings, little touches that show He wants us to not just exist but be thrilled with life. Sunsets over the ocean, sunrise on snowy mountain peaks, clear rushing streams—all evidence of the beauty in creation. He has given His people good things that bring joy: community, family, good jobs, happy moments—they are all from Him.

On the night before He would be crucified, Jesus said this to His disciples: "I have told you these things so that you will be filled with my joy. Yes, your joy will overflow!" (John 15:11 NLT). While this wasn't a moment of happy sunsets, Jesus promised joy to the disciples. The next season of their lives would be filled with darkness and tragedy as they watched their teacher go to the cross, and yet three days later their darkness would break and joy return because of the truth of His resurrection. No matter what we are facing, or how concerned we might be by what we see going on around us, Jesus offers us a joyful outlook because He has risen and we are never alone.

Skeptics of Christianity say things like, "God wants to restrict our enjoyment," or, "He takes away all our freedoms." These whispered lies of the Enemy do not depict the beauty of God's intention for His people. What sad misconceptions! Clearly, they have never met the God of the Bible I have come to know. God gave us the five senses so we could see, hear, smell, taste, and touch the creation and drink it all in. In Old Testament times, the Law was a joy to God's people, never a duty, because it was a path to an exhilarating life not constricted by the weight of sin and guilt. In Christ, there is unspeakable joy!

I doubt Paul would have penned these words were he not convinced by his own experience that they were actually possible: "Do not be anxious about anything, but in every situation, by prayer and petition, with thanksgiving, present your requests to God.

And the peace of God, which transcends all understanding, will guard your hearts and your minds in Christ Jesus" (Phil. 4:6–7). In a world plagued by anxiety, depression, and addiction, it is comforting to know that God not only cares but offers a remedy—not necessarily a quick fix, but a means to address anxiety when it rears its head. Just one more way God shows His desire for our flourishing.

Read below a small sampling of the 7,487 promises God makes to mankind recorded in the Bible, and note what images of God come to mind as you hear them. God promises His followers:

1. Personal knowledge of God: "Therefore the Lord himself will give you a sign. Behold, the virgin shall conceive and bear a son, and shall call his name Immanuel [which means, God with us]" (Isa. 7:14 ESV).

Why has every ancient civilization ever discovered been found to have had idols and statues they fashioned to give them an image of a god to worship? It is because we know innately that we are the result of a Creator and, therefore, we yearn to not only know what He is like, but to actually know Him. Idols give people pictures (albeit distorted) of a god to which they can relate. But these idols are not alive; they have no power. The longing of an idol-worshipper to connect with the true God is never quenched.

In the opening paragraph of the Gospel of John, the apostle writes, "The Word became flesh and made his dwelling among us. . . . No one has ever seen God, but the one and only Son, who is himself God and is in closest relationship with the Father, has made him known" (John 1:14a, 18). Jesus is not a graven image of

God; He is God. God didn't just provide a picture of Himself, He literally provided Himself in Christ. Because of Jesus, no one ever again needs to wonder what God is like, what His character is, or what He wants from us. God became personal so we can know Him intimately.

In Mark 3, Jesus ascends a mountainside and calls twelve men to be His inner circle of disciples from His throng of followers. As is fitting for their commissioning, Jesus lays out what their mission will entail: "He appointed twelve that they might be with him and that he might send them out to preach and to have authority to drive out demons" (Mark 3:14–15). While we know their ministry in subsequent years would be nothing short of incredible, I suspect the first part of this mission statement would be the one most dear to them—just to "be with him."

All their lives these men had followed Jewish teachings to various degrees in an attempt to understand God. Now they are eating, fishing, and traveling with Jesus, participating in miracles and getting to know Jesus in a deeply personal way. They have unfettered access to the God of Abraham, Moses, and David. No greater privilege had ever been bestowed on man. And if it's all true—if Jesus truly has made a way for us to be made right with God—then we, too, are granted access to the Father through the Son today. We, too, can know God in a personal way through Jesus Christ.

This personal relationship with God affects every aspect of our lives. Specifically, consider how it impacts how we pray. We don't need to wonder what or who is on the other end of our prayers—we know Him! With Jesus, prayer becomes a conversation as with an intimate friend. As we get to know Him better, we start not only speaking with Him conversationally when we pray, but we often hear Him speak to us in a still, quiet voice. This is the work of the promised Holy Spirit.

2. The Holy Spirit: "And I will ask the Father, and he will give you another advocate to help you and be with you forever—the Spirit of truth" (John 14:16–17a).

The Holy Spirit is the third and least understood member of the Trinity because He seems a bit more mysterious, but He is no less active throughout Scripture than the Father and Son.

Here are just a few functions of the Holy Spirit in the life of a believer:

- *He teaches us all things.*
  ". . . the Holy Spirit, whom the Father will send in my name, will teach you all things and will remind you of everything I have said to you." (John 14:26)
- *He is a source of revelation.*
  "These are the things God has revealed to us by his Spirit. The Spirit searches all things, even the deep things of God. For who knows a person's thoughts except their own spirit within them? In the same way no one knows the thoughts of God except the Spirit of God." (1 Cor. 2:10–11)

- *He empowers us to witness.*

   "But you will receive power when the Holy Spirit comes on you; and you will be my witnesses in Jerusalem, and in all Judea and Samaria, and to the ends of the earth." (Acts 1:8)

- *He bestows us with gifts to edify the church and cultivate good in society.*

   "Now to each one the manifestation of the Spirit is given for the common good. To one there is given through the Spirit a message of wisdom, to another a message of knowledge by means of the same Spirit, to another faith by the same Spirit, to another gifts of healing by that one Spirit, to another miraculous powers, to another prophecy, to another distinguishing between spirits, to another speaking in different kinds of tongues, and to still another the interpretation of tongues. All these are the work of one and the same Spirit, and he distributes them to each one, just as he determines." (1 Cor. 12:7–11)

- *He patiently transforms our character to be like Jesus.*

   "And we all, who with unveiled faces contemplate the Lord's glory, are being transformed into his image with

> ever-increasing glory, which comes from the
> Lord, who is the Spirit." (2 Cor. 3:18)

This verse (and many others!) speaks of our sanctification, which is the process of becoming a little more like Jesus each day on our road to being pure and perfect, which will be complete when we reach heaven (glorification). If any living organism ceases to grow it begins to die, but God has given the Spirit, who continually cultivates growth in the life of His people. He is sanctifying us, growing us each day a little more into the image of Jesus. What a gift!

3. His personal presence always: Jesus's last words to His disciples were, "I am with you always" (Matt. 28:20).

The resurrection of Jesus assures us He is alive and at work today as much as ever before. This is why Easter is one of the greatest celebrations of the year, and ultimately why Christmas is worth celebrating. He isn't just God entering into our everyday world, but God willing to sacrifice His life on the cross so that we might be with Him always. Jesus invites His followers into relationship with Him and pledges to never leave us nor forsake us (Deut. 31:6). He promises to stand by our side from here to eternity. There is nothing we can do to make Jesus love us any more or any less, and nothing we can do that would convince Him to leave us.

4. Forgiveness of sins: Guilt is a crippling emotion. Psychiatrist offices are filled with people exhibiting various manifestations of guilt. There is a universal moral code imbedded in our DNA that, when violated, causes us to feel shame and remorse. We want to alleviate guilt, so we either hide from the person we violated, or we humble ourselves, apologize, and make restitution. This is the model for guilt incurred by wronging other people, but wronging God is far graver. "The wages of sin is death" (Rom. 6:23a), and we all rightly deserve this punishment because we have all sinned. This is a penalty we cannot pay ourselves because we don't have a righteous life to give to make things right. It could only be paid for us by God taking on flesh and living a sin-free life, then taking our punishment on the cross. The rest of Romans 6:23 reads: "but the gift of God is eternal life in Christ Jesus our Lord."

Imagine what it felt like for God the Father to see His Son in torment on the cross knowing He was completely innocent. Imagine the anguish in Jesus that led Him to cry out, "My God, my God, why have you forsaken me?" (Matt. 27:46). For the first and only time in Jesus's life, He had to experience separation from His Father. This is sin's just consequence. But had Jesus not been willing to take our sin on Himself, we would be left to live separated from God's presence, His will, and His goodness all our lives and into eternity. Sadly, this is the plight of those who never surrender their lives to Jesus.

How freeing to have the weight of guilt removed, once and for all, never to return! God spoke through the Old Testament prophet Jeremiah, saying, "I will forgive their wickedness and will remember their sins no more" (Jer. 31:34b). Through Christ, our sins are forgiven and forgotten. Through Christ, we have right standing with God because, when He looks at us, He sees His Son. Even after trusting Christ, we will continue to err this side of heaven, but the punishment for us has already been paid by God

Himself. So when we come to God remorsefully and say, "God, I'm sorry, but I did it again," He replies, "Did what?"

5. A new identity: God gives His people the privilege of becoming the children of God: "See what great love the Father has lavished on us, that we should be called children of God! And that is what we are!" (1 John 3:1a).

The apostle Peter gives us this assurance: "Praise be to the God and Father of our Lord Jesus Christ! In his great mercy he has given us new birth into a living hope through the resurrection of Jesus Christ from the dead, and into an inheritance that can never perish, spoil or fade" (1 Pet. 1:3–4a).

What is required to become a child of God? Fortunately, it is not an arduous undertaking. God has done all the heavy lifting: "Yet to all who did receive him [Jesus], to those who believed in his name, he gave the right to become children of God—children born not of natural descent, nor of human decision or a husband's will, but born of God" (John 1:12–13). God offers us redemption as a gift provided by Jesus on the cross. To receive Jesus simply means to accept His gift, embrace forgiveness from the penalty of sin, and receive Him into our heart as Lord. And how? We must surrender our lives to Him. It's not that we simply believe in Him, but that we surrender to Him, putting Him in the seat of authority in our lives rather than ourselves. It is as simple as expressing your desire in a prayer like this: "Jesus, I love You. I have sinned and done what is evil in Your sight. Thank You for dying in my place and taking on the penalty for my sins. I give You my life and commit to follow You every step of the way. I receive You as Lord."

To believe requires a bit more explanation. In the previous verse, the apostle John is not merely referring to belief the way our Western ears hear it, like, "I believe my car is blue." I have great faith it's blue. In fact, I think I could convince you my car is blue. However, that belief has very little impact on how I live.

The Greek word John chose for *believe* is the verb πιστεύω (pronounced pisteúō), which means firm conviction or to fully trust with everything we have. This form of belief should motivate our every thought, word, and action. It should permeate every fabric of our lives. It should be our true north and define our purpose for living. It should wake us in the morning and spark a prayer of thanks as we fall asleep.

This is why the title of this book is so poignant. If it's all true, then nothing else in this world could ever be as significant or life-impacting. If it's all true, then we must live under the authority of that truth. Jesus either becomes our all in all, or He should be nothing to us at all. There is no legitimate, intellectually viable middle ground.

6. A fruitful life: "Blessed is the one who trusts in the LORD, whose confidence is in him. They will be like a tree planted by the water that sends out its roots by the stream. It does not fear when heat comes; its leaves are always green. It has no worries in a year of drought and never fails to bear fruit" (Jer. 17:7–8).

As we age, we hear more talk about two words: *legacy* and *eulogy*. We don't get to decide when to be born or when to die, but we have great control over how we steward the time in between.

Linda Ellis wrote a famous poem about the dash between our birth year and death:

> For it matters not how much we own,
> The cars, the house, the cash.
> What matters is how we live and love
> And how we spend our dash.[31]

How are we making a difference in the world, especially to those we care about most? How will we be remembered after our death? We feel pride when our work benefits other people. What motivates teachers, police, and firefighters to work so hard for marginal pay? They want to make a difference. To put it in agrarian terms, they want to bear fruit with their lives. This desire is yet another consistent element in our human DNA. We want to live a fruitful life.

Jesus used a familiar picture to instruct His agrarian-minded disciples: "I am the vine; you are the branches. If you remain in me and I in you, you will bear much fruit; apart from me you can do nothing. . . . This is to my Father's glory, that you bear much fruit, showing yourselves to be my disciples" (John 15:5, 8).

What kind of fruit pleases the Lord (and fulfills us)? We have a cornucopia from which to choose!

- There is the fruit of evangelism—introducing others to the eternal life Jesus offers.
- The fruit of righteousness—doing right things that benefit not only us but also our community.

- The fruit of justice—giving shape to culture by calling out what is wrong and pointing to truth.
- The fruit of loving others—reflecting God's love for the unlovable, the downcast, and dejected as well as our neighbors, friends, and family members.

In Jesus, we experience the fulfillment of producing fruit that is enjoyed by many.

7. Authentic community: "Every day they continued to meet together in the temple courts. They broke bread in their homes and ate together with glad and sincere hearts" (Acts 2:46).

Social media has shown us how much we desire to know and be known, and yet, it also is why most people today under forty are starved for authentic community. They are present in a digital space, even a crowd of followers, yet they feel so alone. True community is found with people willing to empathize with our concerns, celebrate our triumphs, and mourn our griefs. We connect with them at a heart level.

The followers of Jesus knew full well that, apart from Jesus, they were lost and broken. So, they chose to share honestly and encourage one another in their pursuit of righteousness. The author of the letter to the Hebrews exhorted this young church to "consider how we may spur one another on toward love and good deeds, not giving up meeting together, as some are in the habit of doing, but encouraging one another—and all the more as you see the Day approaching" (Heb. 10:24–25). This kind of community can only be found with God's people in the church, one of God's kindest gifts to His people. This is one of the attractions to churches today—a community of friends supporting one another in the pursuit of similar noble goals.

Two famous men from the Old Testament had what might be called a covenant friendship: "Jonathan became one in spirit with David, and he loved him as himself. . . . And Jonathan made a covenant with David" (1 Sam. 18:1b, 3a). Other phrases like "steadfast love" and "dealt kindly" were used to further describe their friendship—one characterized by enduring faithfulness and unwavering commitment. Does this sound attractive to you?

In my work with Young Life, I have known many teens who were buddies growing up, and then Christ came into their lives around the same time. I watched as they transitioned from being buddies to brothers or sisters in Christ. When one would go off to a party, the other would go along to hold them accountable to not drink. Or when one was trying out for a sports team, the other would work out with them, track their times, and pray for them on the day of tryouts. Later, these friends would stand as attendants in each other's weddings. Whether we're in a hard or relatively easy season of life, it feels great to know we aren't navigating it alone. Not only do we have the Lord of Life with us, we have brothers and sisters committed to our thriving.

I am fortunate to have such a friend in my life named John Colston. We have been great friends since the seventh grade. And fortuitously, we both began a relationship with Jesus around the same time in high school as a result of our involvement in Young

Life. After college, John moved to Princeton, New Jersey, and was working there. I joined the staff of Young Life and was sent to begin work in Oakton, Virginia. Once I was offered a full-time roll there, John quit his job and moved to Oakton to live and volunteer with me in this ministry. His gifts are the perfect complement to mine. I count it one of life's richest privileges to walk with a brother through the many seasons of life!

Authentic community is grounded in love for neighbor and it's in the church among God's people that covenant friendship may be found. The Bible instructs us to live as people who love well: "Dear friends, let us love one another, for love comes from God. Everyone who loves has been born of God and knows God" (1 John 4:7). When we are loved, we need not hide our faults or try to impress—we can be our authentic selves. Rather than being filled with anxiety, we can lean into every facet of life with peace and optimism—and that is good news and a good gift from God!

8. Eternal life: The most often quoted verse in the Bible is John 3:16: "For God so loved the world that he gave his one and only Son, that whoever believes in him shall not perish but have eternal life." Jesus did all the work—everything that was required—so we might be afforded eternal life with Him. That life begins when you commit to Him and carries into eternity. But this gift is not mandated or forced on anyone; it is just available to those who believe and receive Him.

Through the lens of eternity our few decades here on the earth are a mere blip on the radar screen. The gift of eternal life changes our perspective, our priorities, and draws us to follow

Jesus through this life and into the next. Jesus told His disciples, "Whoever serves me must follow me; and where I am, my servant also will be. My Father will honor the one who serves me" (John 12:26).

"The world and its desires pass away, but whoever does the will of God lives forever" (1 John 2:17).

9. A mission to change the world: "Go into all the world and proclaim the gospel to the whole creation. Whoever believes and is baptized will be saved, but whoever does not believe will be condemned" (Mark 16:15–16 ESV).

The legacy Jesus conferred upon His followers dwarfs any other accomplishment I can name. No invention or feat of brilliance has impacted the world more than the Great Commission carried out through the power of the Spirit. Literally billions of people have been brought from death to eternal life because of the faithfulness of Christ's followers, and His followers have been responsible for so much good—from community engagement to hospital care to the building of schools. Christ's impact reverberates throughout our world.

God gives good gifts to His people, but we aren't after the gifts—we're after God Himself. He is the prize. I hope you invite Jesus into your heart because you feel loved and desire to walk with that love forever. Jesus's death and resurrection allow His followers absolute forgiveness of sins, the assurance of eternal life, the free gift of His Spirit, unfettered access to God the Father, and a mission to impact the world for good.[32] Who wants in?

Discuss and Reflect

1. Which of the nine things God promises His followers did you find most attractive? Why do you think that is?

2. Do you have a hard time believing any of these promises are true for you?

3. What does truly authentic community look like? Do you have friends who fill this need for you? If not, how might you seek this?

4. Does being a part of the Great Commission intimidate you or motivate you?

11

What If It's True That Jesus Rose from the Dead—Then What?

> "If Jesus rose from the dead, then you have to accept all that
> he said. If he didn't, then why worry about any of what he
> said? The issue on which everything hangs is not whether
> you like his teaching, but whether he rose from the dead."
> TIM KELLER, *THE REASON FOR GOD*[33]

According to eyewitness accounts in the Bible, as well as extrabiblical references, Jesus of Nazareth died on a cross, was buried, and then resurrected three days later. The Scriptures note Jesus visited several of His followers, including five hundred people on a single occasion. Soon, word spread that Jesus had risen from the dead. In considering if the resurrection of Jesus is a two-thousand-year-old legend or factual event, we must take into account the number of eyewitness testimonies and other verifiable historical evidence.

Everything Jesus taught and claimed depended on His resurrection from the dead. If Jesus didn't rise as He promised, His message of forgiveness and hope for eternal life would be meaningless. Why? Because seven hundred years before Christ, the prophet Isaiah prophesied about a future Messiah who would die for sins but later be restored to life. Jesus quoted from Isaiah 53 to assure His disciples that He was, in fact, this Messiah, and that He would die for the sins of the world and rise again: "'We are going up to Jerusalem,' he said, 'and the Son of Man will be delivered over to the chief priests and the teachers of the law. They will condemn him to death and will hand him over to the Gentiles, who will mock him and spit on him, flog him and kill him. Three days later he will rise'" (Mark 10:33–34).

The resurrection, therefore, is one of the pinnacle markers for the Messiah. Bible scholar Wilbur Smith explains, "When Jesus said He would rise again from the dead, the third day after He was crucified, He said something that only a fool would dare say if He expected the devotion of any disciples—unless He was sure He was going to rise!"[34]

In John chapter 2, we find the familiar account of Jesus entering the temple market and being quite displeased by what He finds. Vendors had turned the outer courts of the temple into an open market selling birds and other items required for religious cleansing. Jesus flips the tables of the vendors and money changers to demonstrate He has authority even over the religious traditions of the past. "The Jews then responded to him, 'What sign can you show us to prove your authority to do all this?' Jesus answered them, 'Destroy this temple, and I will raise it again in three days'" (John 2:18–19). Clearly, the proof of Jesus's messiahship, according to Him, was the resurrection. If there were no resurrection, Christianity would have died out at the cross when the disciples fled for their lives. Instead, a worldwide movement was launched that continues to spread today!

Josephus was a first-century Jewish historian who made some powerful references to Jesus and to His resurrection in his writings called *The Antiquities of the Jews*. One of his references says,

> About this time there lived Jesus, a wise man, if indeed one ought to call him a man. For he . . . wrought surprising feats. . . . He was the Christ. When Pilate . . . condemned him to be crucified, those who had . . . come to love him did not give up their affection for him. On the third day he appeared . . . restored to life. . . . And the tribe of Christians . . . has . . . not disappeared.[35]

The fact that Josephus was a Jew yet he could not downplay the significance of Jesus and the movement He started (the church), speaks to the validity of these peoples' belief in their resurrected Lord.

Pontius Pilate was the governor of Judea who allowed the crucifixion of Jesus. After Jesus breathed His last, Pilate wanted to

verify that Jesus was, in fact, dead. To put an end to any specula-
tion, he commanded a Roman guard to thrust a spear into Jesus's
side after He had already hung on the cross for six hours. The
mixture of blood and water that flowed, again according to the
eyewitnesses who recorded this in the Gospels, certified His death.
Jesus's body was taken down from the cross, tightly wrapped in
linen, and buried in Joseph of Arimathea's tomb. A Roman guard
was assigned to guard the tomb around the clock. Historians differ on the exact number in such a guard, but they agree it was
between sixteen and sixty trained men. Failure would mean certain death to the guards, so it is nearly impossible Jesus's body was
stolen by His disciples or anyone else.

In John chapter 20, we read of two separate occasions when
Jesus walked into a room where His disciples were holed up. "The
disciples were overjoyed when they saw the Lord" (v. 20), but
Thomas was missing on the first occasion and famously said he
would not believe until he saw and touched the nail holes in Jesus's
hands for himself (vv. 24–25). So, Jesus came back: "A week later
his disciples were in the house again, and Thomas was with them.
Though the doors were locked, Jesus came and stood among them
and said, 'Peace be with you!' Then he said to Thomas, 'Put your
finger here; see my hands. Reach out your hand and put it into my
side. Stop doubting and believe.' Thomas said to him, 'My Lord
and my God!'" (vv. 26–28).

Why do you think the disciples were so "overjoyed" to see
the risen Lord? Was it just because they missed their friend? I'm
sure that is true; however, the bigger reason is because Jesus's

resurrection was the ultimate proof that it was all true—that Jesus was who He had claimed to be all along. He is truly the promised Messiah to whom they can confidently surrender their lives.

Something extraordinary resulted from these appearances. These bewildered followers of Jesus ceased mourning and began to boldly proclaim Jesus was alive. These former cowards were suddenly willing to suffer humiliation, torture, and death. They risked everything for the sake of continuing Jesus's mission. They not only would, but did, give their life to spread the truth. No one would die for a lie. All except two disciples were slain as martyrs, never refusing the truth of Jesus's resurrection, even when it meant they'd be sawn in two.

> That which was from the beginning, which we have heard, which we have seen with our eyes, which we have looked at and our hands have touched—this we proclaim concerning the Word of life. The life appeared; we have seen it and testify to it, and we proclaim to you the eternal life, which was with the Father and has appeared to us. We proclaim to you what we have seen and heard, so that you also may have fellowship with us. And our fellowship is with the Father and with his Son, Jesus Christ. We write this to make our joy complete. (1 John 1:1–4)

Here is the bottom line: we must choose what we believe about Jesus's resurrection because it is the hinge point of the gospel and the Bible itself. It is the hinge point of history! If Jesus truly rose from the grave, then it is *all* true, and the only responsible action is to surrender our lives to Him. If Jesus rose from the dead, then He is the ultimate authority on life and He is worthy of our worship. So when He says, "I am the way and the truth and the life. No one comes to the Father except through me" (John 14:6), we must listen.

Discuss and Reflect

1. How do you feel about the evidence surrounding the resurrection of Jesus? Do you believe it happened?

2. Why did Jesus need to rise from the dead to fulfill His role as the long-awaited Messiah?

3. What is the significance of the resurrection for you personally? What difference has it made in your life?

12

Do Painful Experiences
Nullify What Is True?

Why does God allow bad things to happen?" is, surprisingly, a recent question in the span of history. For millennia, suffering was so normal that it was just another part of life, not a problem to be solved. Chris Goswami says it this way: "In developed economies we are shielded from much of the suffering that occurred in the past. For example, until the 18th century, people expected one in three of their children to die before they reached the age of 5, and mothers regularly died in childbirth. Pestilence, hunger, and plague came around often, and, if you made it through all that, your life expectancy was only 40."[36]

Today, medical technology has benefitted millions, reducing pain and extending life. But it has also brought the expectation that we shouldn't have to suffer, or at least if we go through hard things, there's some anesthesia so we don't have to feel the pain.

So, when things go wrong, we end up asking, "Why?" The Bible depicts a God who works powerfully in and through suffering to draw us to Himself. He is not the author of hardship, but He does hold authority over it.

In John 11, we encounter a grieving Martha angry that Jesus hadn't come sooner to heal her brother, Lazarus, who had just died. Yet her pain drove her to come to Jesus. Like labor pains before the joy of birth, suffering can serve as an entry point to a deep, abiding, trusting, and personal relationship with the living Lord. If, as Jesus claims, the goal of our existence is a loving relationship with Him, finding Him in our suffering serves this purpose.

There is a lot of theology around the problem of suffering, but it's enough to note just three things:

First, *Christians believe disasters, sickness, even accidents, were never part of God's original creation*. The garden of Eden depicts a good and perfect place: "God saw all that he had made, and it was very good" (Gen. 1:31a). It was when Adam and Eve sinned that hardship and suffering entered the world.

God did not create robots, but human beings with the freedom to choose and act as we desire. I know it is foolish to drive my car over one hundred miles per hour, but if I want to, I can. God didn't put a governor on my car to restrict my ability to speed, nor has He put a governor on our lives that keeps us from sinning. He is honored when we freely choose to obey Him.

Obviously, there are both natural and spiritual consequences to our choices. Some natural consequences of speeding are accidents, injury, a ticket, even death. Some spiritual consequences for turning our back on what God says are anxiety, strained relation-ships, guilt, unanswered prayer, frustration, lack of purpose—this list goes on and on. We've all tasted one or more of these person-ally at some point, and the taste is bitter.

Sin and its consequences have brought suffering into our world, but it was not the intended design. God's heart for His people is that they would flourish, not flounder, and He has made a way to return to His good design.

Second, *suffering has no part in God's final creation.* At the crucifixion God defeated evil, suffering, and death itself. These victories are the firstfruits of what is to come for all who trust Him. At the fulfillment of this age "'. . . there will be no more death' or mourning or crying or pain" (Rev. 21:4a). Right now, however, we live between the ages—the already and the not yet— between Genesis and Revelation, in a disfigured world that is not as it should be.

We sometimes imagine God to be distant and disconnected. We think, "If only He would wave His magic wand, the bad things would go away." But it's not like that. God is neither distant nor unconcerned about suffering. We see glimpses of the not yet in the way God never leaves us to face suffering alone. God accompanies us and has a personal knowledge of suffering and loss. God said, "Never will I leave you; never will I forsake you" (Heb. 13:5), and one day we will both dwell with Him and be free from suffering for all of eternity.

Third, *Christianity is the only faith that has the suffering and death of its own God at its core.* "Consider him who endured such opposition from sinners, so that you will not grow weary and lose heart" (Heb. 12:3). Unlike any of the world religions around us, we have a God who took on flesh "and dwelt among us" (John 1:14 CSB). He has walked the path of suffering in a human body, and we know He both understands our pain and has ultimately defeated it.

The Bible begins and ends with happiness, but the meat of the story is raw. We are not promised there won't be sadness in the interim. What end could possibly be worth all this pain? Jesus says He is. He is the prize.

The apostle Peter reminds us of the importance of viewing life through an eternal lens. If our focus is only on the here and now, then suffering seems like an unbearable trauma—one that causes us to miss our chance for joy. But if our purpose is to glorify God and reflect His nature to others, then suffering and how we handle it can have purpose. This is not to say that God ordains all suffering. Most of the suffering we face is the result of a sin-filled, broken world. We reap what we sow, and we are the recipients of what others sow as well. It's because of Christ and His victorious death and resurrection that we can walk with faith and strength through suffering, knowing eternal peace is coming: "Dear friends, do not be surprised at the fiery ordeal that has come on you to test you, as though something strange were happening to you. But rejoice inasmuch as you participate in the sufferings of Christ, so that you may be overjoyed when his glory is revealed" (1 Pet. 4:12–13).

As we close this chapter, it's important to remind ourselves of a question we often forget: Why does God allow good things to happen? Why should there be mountain views, days at the seaside, job satisfaction, the joy of children, a welcoming smile, or an ice cream sundae? God doesn't owe us any of this. And why do many bad things *not* happen—that virus you didn't catch, the accident you narrowly avoided? There is no guaranteed ticket to a life free from harm. It's tempting to think that if we pray, pursue good works, and give away our money, we are owed smooth sailing, but God hasn't promised that.

A well-developed attitude of wonder at creation, and gratefulness to God for all that is right, can underpin our lives. And perhaps it can provide us with some balance when we enter those hardest of times: "Rejoice always, pray continually, give thanks in all circumstances; for this is God's will for you in Christ Jesus" (1 Thess. 5:16–18).

Discuss and Reflect

1. Did God intend for mankind to suffer? If not, why do we?

2. How did suffering come about?

3. In what ways can God use suffering for a good purpose?

4. Do you feel like Jesus can relate to our suffering? Why or why not?

13

How Do We Turn Our Lives Over to Jesus?

Jesus said, "Here I am! I stand at the door and knock. If anyone hears my voice and opens the door, I will come in and eat with that person, and they with me" (Rev. 3:20).

I hope it is clear by now that God the Son did not become a man simply to teach us how to act or paint living pictures of what true religion should look like. No, He came so we could truly know God, not just know about Him. He came so that we could have a personal relationship with God, walking with Him each day, because He removed the barrier between us and God that was put in place by sin. This is life's most compelling privilege! Those who trust God are His children with abundant purpose and the key to finding life's purpose! It is also the key to eternal life in heaven. Some of you have likely responded to the invitation to follow Jesus, while others are still contemplating that decision. My intent in this chapter is twofold: first, to clarify how one turns their life over to Jesus; second, to help believers see how they can share this invitation with seekers in their network.

What is required of us to become a new creation in Christ? The debt we owed has already been paid; we must only respond. These three action verbs fairly represent the New Testament's teaching on this question:

1. *Believe*

> "I write these things to you who believe in the name of the Son of God so that you may know that you have eternal life." (1 John 5:13)

> As mentioned in chapter 10, the Greek word here for *believe* does not mean just to accept as true. It's not just an exercise of the mind. Instead, it means to be so convinced of the truth of the gospel that one surrenders every aspect of their life to Jesus. True belief is seen in active trust, in obedience. In essence, we hand back the deed of our lives to our Creator and ask Him to do as He likes with us, knowing His ways are good and just.

2. *Repent*

> "The people living in darkness have seen a great light; on those living in

the land of the shadow of death a
light has dawned. From that time
on Jesus began to preach, 'Repent,
for the kingdom of heaven has come
near.'" (Matt. 4:16–17)

The Greek word for *repent* means to turn
around or change one's direction. Theologian
R. C. Sproul popularized a Latin phrase that
encapsulates the result of our turning toward
God. It is *Coram Deo,* which simply means
"living before the face of God."[37] When we
repent, we turn away from our own ways
that lead to death and do a one-eighty so that
we now face God. Our backs were to Him
while we chased our own desires, but when
we repent, we turn and sprint back to the
One whose way leads to life. We surrender
to Him, asking forgiveness for our sins and
redemption for our souls, and He is faithful
to not only forgive, but to forget, and to walk
with us every day.

3. *Follow*

"'Come, follow me,' Jesus said, 'and I
will send you out to fish for people.'"
(Matt. 4:19)

> Jesus invites us to "follow" Him,
> walking with Him in the direction He leads.
> It means saying yes to Him, and no when
> our way conflicts with His. We gladly say
> yes because we trust Him more than we
> trust ourselves, knowing His way is always
> higher and better. The more we get to know
> the Lord, the easier it becomes to obey His
> teaching. Experience proves Him right every
> time!

As we follow Jesus, we become more and more like Him. This makes us a radiant example to those with whom we interact. We look forward to telling the story of what God has done in our life and sharing Jesus with others. The Holy Spirit will show each of us how to fish, or share the good news about Jesus, in a manner that fits our unique personality. Most people today resist someone preaching at them. But people with whom we are in relationship enjoy hearing our stories, what makes us tick, and what is important to us. So sharing our journey with Jesus is not preaching, but enjoying a shared life together.

In 1 Corinthians 15, Paul gives us a concise yet beautiful summary of the gospel story—the centerpiece of our faith:

> Now, brothers and sisters, I want to remind
> you of the gospel I preached to you, which you
> received and on which you have taken your
> stand. By this gospel you are saved, if you hold

firmly to the word I preached to you. Otherwise, you have believed in vain.

For what I received I passed on to you as of first importance: that Christ died for our sins according to the Scriptures, that he was buried, that he was raised on the third day according to the Scriptures, and that he appeared to Cephas [Peter], and then to the Twelve. After that, he appeared to more than five hundred of the brothers and sisters at the same time, most of whom are still living, though some have fallen asleep. (vv. 1–6)

The Bridge illustration, developed by the Navigators ministry, depicts the chief points of the gospel message. Mankind is separated from God by our sin, illustrated by the chasm that is infinitely wide and cannot be crossed by our own effort. Christ's death on the cross is the bridge by which we enter into fellowship with God and become a new creation. We are saved by God's grace, not by our works. Good works flow naturally from our new heart aligned with His.[38]

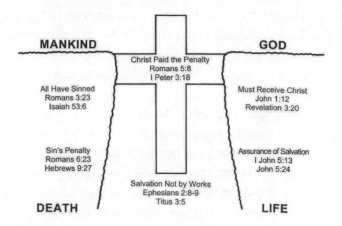

Jesus tells a parable of a prodigal son recorded in the fifteenth chapter of Luke, and it illustrates God's heart for sinners beautifully. A wealthy landowner had two sons. One of them decided he no longer wanted to live under his father's roof or by his rules (This should sound familiar to any parents of teenagers!), so he took his inheritance and spent it on "wild living" in a foreign land. When he had squandered the entirety of his inheritance, he found himself destitute, caring for pigs, and dreaming of eating their food. Then the key verse comes: "When he came to his senses . . ." (v. 17) he returned to his father.

What does it mean that "he came to his senses?" It means this lost son was confronted by his brokenness and need for help. He yearned for fellowship with his family and friends. Perhaps the Spirit of God prompted him to return to his good father. As a result, this son repented, making the long trip back, hoping his father would at least let him stay as a servant in his household. Instead, here's the father's response: "While he was still a long way off, his father saw him and was filled with compassion for him; *he ran to his son*, threw his arms around him and kissed him" (v. 20, emphasis added).

The son cried out to his father, "I have sinned against heaven and against you. I am no longer worthy to be called your son" (v. 21). But the father cut him off mid-sentence and yelled to his servants, "'Quick! Bring the best robe and put it on him. Put a ring on his finger and sandals on his feet. Bring the fattened calf and kill it. Let's have a feast and celebrate. For this son of mine was dead and is alive again; he was lost and is found.' So they began to celebrate" (vv. 22–24). This is God's response to each person who repents and returns to His loving arms.

He doesn't just welcome the sinner home. He celebrates over him, reconciling him to a right relationship through the work of Jesus on the cross, who paid our ransom and rescued us from sin and death by laying down His life for us. Our sin separated us from God, but Jesus made a way to be together again, and His work on the cross was sufficient for this work—our redemption.

Allow these Scriptures to give you assurance:

- "Truly, truly, I say to you, whoever hears my word and believes him who sent me has eternal life. He does not come into judgment, but has passed from death to life." (John 5:24 ESV)

- "I write these things to you who believe in the name of the Son of God, that you may know that you have eternal life." (1 John 5:13 ESV)

If you are reading today, and you've never given your life to Jesus and are ready to surrender to Him, know that the Lord awaits you with open arms. He invites you to pray in your own words, telling Him of your belief that Jesus is indeed the Messiah and of your desire to follow Him all the days of your life. If the Spirit is calling you to surrender today, don't turn the page until you respond to Him. Reach out to a friend who knows Jesus or to your pastor to let them know about the decision you are making. They can help guide you.

Some of you may be feeling that you have drifted apart from your first love and need to rededicate yourself to following Jesus. Others may feel that now, for the first time, you are ready to surrender your life to the One who died to redeem you. In either case, the Lord awaits your return, which begins with a prayer in your own words similar to this one:

Dear Jesus, I believe with all my heart that You are truly God in a man, the promised Messiah. I repent for having lived life on my own terms, and I turn the keys to my life over to You. You purchased all of me, and I am so very grateful for Your sacrifice of love shown on the cross. I commit to follow You each day, trusting Your ways are far better than mine.

Come into my life, Holy Spirit, that I may grow more and more into the image of my Savior. Amen.

This prayer is not the end goal but rather the starting line of our sanctification—the process of growing into the image of Jesus. It is important we find a church and community of believers who can spur us on in our journey with Jesus and offer us opportunities to engage our gifts in kingdom service.

I want to close this chapter by mentioning an important occurrence that takes place when we surrender our lives to Jesus. Scripture tells us we are given the Holy Spirit to live in our hearts and help guide us along in our journey:

> "If you love me, you will keep my commandments. And I will ask the Father, and he will give you another Helper, to be with you forever, even the Spirit of truth, whom the world cannot receive, because it neither sees him nor knows him. You know him, for he dwells with you and will be in you. . . . the Helper, the Holy Spirit, whom the Father will send in my name, he will teach you all things and bring to your remembrance all that I have said to you." (John 14:15–17, 26 ESV)

There are volumes of books written about the Holy Spirit, but here are just three of the Spirit's functions we can look forward to experiencing:

1. **Wisdom:** We see God at work in our lives and in the world. For the wise person, the wonders of nature, historical events, and our everyday experiences are now seen through a kingdom perspective.

2. **Counsel (right judgment):** The gift of counsel allows us to know the difference between right and wrong, and we are strengthened to do what is right. A person with right judgment avoids sin and lives out the values taught by Jesus.

3. **Courage:** The gift of courage helps us overcome our fears and walk in faith. We're given courage to stand for what is right in the sight of God, even if it means facing rejection, verbal abuse, or physical harm.

How comforting it is to know that the God of the universe resides in the heart of every believer in the form of the Holy Spirit. In Him, we are never alone!

Discuss and Reflect

1. What does Jesus desire for each of us more than anything else?

2. What did Jesus do to make a personal relationship with Him possible?

3. What three steps are we invited to take to begin this relationship with Jesus? What role of the Holy Spirit do you most look forward to experiencing?

14

How Can I Live a Fully Integrated Life with Jesus?

Hall of Fame college basketball coach John Wooden taught, "The true test of a person's character is what he does when no one is watching."[39] This is the quintessential definition of integrity; that space where our beliefs, words, and actions all intersect, both in public and private.

We are one person, not a collection of multiple personalities. Each of our thoughts, words, and actions flows from the center of our lives, creating what we often call character. And character for those in Christ should resemble the One we follow: Jesus.

How much of our lives do you think Jesus desires to be a part of? Answer: all of it! Romans 5:8 says Jesus came and died for us because He loves us so much. He didn't pay the penalty only to be a part of the "religious" slice of our lives—He wants *all* of us! Listen to this: "The LORD directs the steps of the godly. He delights in every detail of their lives. Though they stumble, they will never fall, for the LORD holds them by the hand" (Ps. 37:23–24 NLT).

Just as we earthly parents are enthralled with everything our kids do, our heavenly Father desires to walk with us through every moment of our day and is completely engaged with us. He is the one who gifted us with our various talents and interests, so wouldn't it make sense that He desires to be a part of our enjoyment of those gifts?

Growing up I was a guy's guy. I was an only child and I spent most of my childhood outdoors playing every sport you can name. Then I got married and we had not one, not two, but three daughters! I was horrified when Kris, my beautiful wife, told me that their dance class was having a recital for parents at the same time as the final round of the Masters Golf Tournament. I coughed and tried to feign a cold, but Kris was not moved. So I painstakingly made my way into the auditorium to see my daughter's two minutes of fame in the midst of three hours of performances from the other child prodigies (who, of course, were nowhere near as talented as my own)!

To my astonishment, seeing my daughter on stage dancing her heart out caused tears of pride to roll down my cheeks. I never missed a recital, sports, or cheer event because my girls were (and still are) the apple of my eye. In an infinitely more profound sense, our heavenly Father is our number-one cheerleader. The problem is we don't always invite Him to the performance.

Our character isn't just seen in the "religious" piece of our lives, but in all that we think, say, and do. Jesus should be the center of our lives—our work, our hobbies, our relationships, all of it! We have the privilege to lead fully integrated lives with our eyes fixed on Jesus, the "author and perfecter" (Heb. 12:2 NASB1995) of life. He is growing us up to be more and more like Him each day, but remember, growing into the man or woman Jesus desires us to be is a process. It does not happen overnight.

Another word for a life centered on Jesus is *righteous*. I shared this definition in chapter 6: the word *righteous* refers to things or systems working according to their intended design. Picture the inside of a computer with its complex makeup of wires, chips, and processors. When all these pieces align and work as intended, it is a righteous system. Righteousness refers to living as we were intended without sin short-circuiting God's intention for us.

Of course, we are all flawed since we're living in a fallen world. No one is perfect. But with God's guidance, we can lay aside many of the hindrances to righteous living and experience a wonderfully fulfilling life. Hebrews 12:1–2a issues this call well: "Therefore, since we are surrounded by such a great cloud of witnesses, let us throw off everything that hinders and the sin that so easily entangles. And let us run with perseverance the race marked out for us, fixing our eyes on Jesus, the pioneer and perfecter of faith."

Joy and Peace, the Fruit of a Fully Integrated Life

The fruit of living with our eyes fixed on Jesus is the possibility for a consistent sense of joy and peace. When we truly know who we are and how much we are loved, we can genuinely be one of those "glass half full" people that livens up any room. It gives us confidence that, despite the challenges we see all around us, things will be okay because the Lord carries us in the palm of His hand. The prophet Isaiah spoke these assuring words for all generations to believe: "You will keep in perfect peace those whose minds are steadfast, because they trust in you" (Isa. 26:3).

When we are in the midst of trials that discourage us, joy is not found by focusing on our current surroundings. Rather, joy is available when we look ahead to the bigger picture and what is to come. It is difficult to imagine anything as horrific as the crucifixion of Jesus, but "for the joy set before him [Jesus] endured the cross" (Heb. 12:2). It was the result to come, His and our future redemption, that allowed Jesus to experience joy in the face of suffering. A kingdom perspective can transform our view of the present, but it takes work.

In speaking of the Lord, King David wrote in Psalm 30, ". . . His favor is for life; Weeping may endure for a night, But joy comes in the morning" (v. 5 NKJV). "If God is for us, who can be against us?" (Rom. 8:31b). We have much for which to be thankful.

Coming out of the Covid-19 pandemic, anxiety was at an all-time high. We were starved for community, stressed about the unknown, and fearful of where that disease would lead. Children were quarantined at home or forced to wear masks in school all day. While there were many somewhat justifiable reasons for a lack of inner peace, God's Word tells us we do not need to accept anxiety as the status quo.

One of Jesus's close companions quotes His illustration of a oxen carrying a load too heavy for a single person as a picture of what He wants to do for us: "Come to me, all you who are weary and burdened, and I will give you rest. Take my yoke upon you and learn from me, for I am gentle and humble in heart, and you will find rest for your souls. For my yoke is easy and my burden is light" (Matt. 11:28–30). The result of having our burdens off-loaded to Jesus is peace and joy. This freedom comes when we commit all that we are to Jesus—to be "yoked" to Him like two oxen working together. We are then free to live unencumbered by the trials of the day as we look toward a bright future.

Jesus laid down His life for His sheep so that we might have peace with God and one another, and it is Jesus who will one day bring everlasting peace to the world when He returns (Rev. 21). The injustice of the world around us can cause us to wonder if Jesus will fulfill His promise. In these times it behooves us to reflect on Jesus as our Good Shepherd and trust that we, His sheep, will one day "dwell in the house of the LORD forever" (Ps. 23:6).

The apostle Peter wrote these instructions for dealing with stress: "Cast all your anxiety on [Jesus] because he cares for you" (1 Pet. 5:7). Would he have written this if it was just a pipe dream? No! He was giving His church instructions for how to practically navigate their lives with Jesus. Since Jesus is interested in every part of our lives—the good *and* the difficult—He, of course, wants to intervene to help alleviate anxiety.

How do we effectively cast our worries on Him? Two steps: First we lift up our concerns to Jesus in prayer. That is the easier of the two steps. The second is to trust that He has not only heard us but is also acting on our behalf. We must look for this response and expect it. Prayer and faith work hand in hand as was shown in the case of Jesus's visit back to His hometown of Nazareth: "He did not do many miracles there because of their lack of faith" (Matt. 13:58). Please don't mishear me and think that, with a proper amount of faith, our every prayer will be answered as we hope. We must be praying for what God's will is, which becomes gradually clearer the more we get to know Him and the more we surrender to His will.

The cost to follow Jesus is the surrender of our will to Him. Jesus said, "If any want to become my followers, let them deny themselves and take up their cross daily and follow me" (Luke 9:23 NRSVA). Taking up our cross refers to dying to ourselves and our will and committing ourselves to obeying His will. God's Word lays out a plan for our flourishing that, when followed, is a blessing to us and those we love.

The word *surrender* brings to mind some pretty negative connotations. Waving the white flag is a sign of defeat and a fearful admission that one is now a prisoner under the charge of another whom they do not respect. Just the opposite is true in the case of surrendering or giving control of our lives to Jesus. We were built to live in complete harmony with our Creator—attached at the hip, so to speak.

In Matthew 13 Jesus shared a parable of what surrendering to Him is like: "Again, the kingdom of heaven is like a merchant in search of fine pearls, who, on finding one pearl of great value, went and sold all that he had and bought it" (vv. 45–46 ESV). We experience joy and peace when we submit to His will and surrender ours. We do this because we trust that He knows what is best for our lives.

To grow in faith, it is important we see Jesus at work. To do so means to give Him chances to show Himself faithful. I know it comes as no surprise that come Monday morning the vast majority of believers cannot remember what was taught at church on Sunday. That is missing the point, don't you think? The average minister spends fifteen to seventeen hours a week preparing their sermon. When we can't recall, what was said, we are squandering their efforts for the gospel to impact our lives.

One effective way to stimulate growth from what is preached is to commit to putting the lesson into practice by asking, "How can I live out this principle this week?" In my ministry with adolescents, we work hard to make the Bible practical and relevant. By challenging students with a measurable action step they can implement each week, they retain the guiding theme of the lesson and actually see the Lord impacting their lives in very practical ways.

One week when I was in high school, my Young Life leader, Marty, did a teaching on the blessing it is to serve others. Then he challenged us to write down the name of someone we would serve that week and report back how it went. I chose my mother, and here is what I did:

As an only child I was never asked to wash the dinner dishes. My mother didn't work outside of the home so she viewed this chore as one of the many ways she could serve our family. But this particular week, my parents had a meeting to run off to right after dinner. That left the dishes undone. "Here is my chance," I thought. I rolled up my sleeves, then washed and put away the dinner dishes. My mother still has heart issues forty-five years later as a result of her shock! I can attest that joy and peace come when we put God's Word to use and when we serve in even the smallest ways. Since this one small act brought such joy and peace, I developed a habit of looking for ways to serve people as an overflow of my life centered on Christ.

Each step of faith we take strengthens our belief that Jesus is alive and well and at work in our life personally, as well as in the world around us. A question to challenge ourselves with is, "What will I do today that I wouldn't do if I didn't believe in Jesus?" Have fun with this one!

Discuss and Reflect

1. Is living a righteous life attractive to you? Why or why not?

2. What are some of the results of living a fully integrated life, putting Jesus first in everything?

3. Which is more important: how we think or how we act?

4. Can you identify a couple of ways you can intentionally put God's Word into practice this week?

15

God Invites His Followers
to Bless and to Lead

In His providence, God gives us a role to play in His work here on Earth. Isn't that humbling to consider? I liken this to being tapped by the president to serve on his or her cabinet—what a privilege, right? In the account of the feeding of the five thousand (recorded in all four Gospels), Jesus invites His fledgling disciples to play a role in this miracle. After Jesus prayed over the loaves of bread and fish, He handed them to the disciples to distribute to the thousands gathered. I can only imagine the astonishment on the disciples' faces as the bread and fish kept expanding to meet the need! What kind of impact do you imagine this had on them down the road?

Could Jesus have pulled off this miraculous feeding without the help of His disciples? Of course, He could have! But He tapped His disciples to give them vision for leading when He would be gone. Leadership is a high privilege, so when we are leading on behalf of Jesus (which every believer is invited to do), we experience a taste of kingdom life here on the earth.

In His famous Sermon on the Mount, Jesus instructed His disciples: "You are the salt of the earth. But if the salt loses its saltiness, how can it be made salty again? It is no longer good for anything, except to be thrown out and trampled underfoot" (Matt. 5:13). The term *salt of the earth* generally refers to a person or group who exhibits noble characteristics worthy of emulation. Salt in biblical times was not only a spice, but also a preservative. Jesus here was likely hinting that His followers would play a role in preserving God's ways in their culture. This meant they would need to see themselves as influencers at all levels of societal life. What an awesome responsibility!

Jesus continued: "You are the light of the world. A town built on a hill cannot be hidden. Neither do people light a lamp and put it under a bowl. Instead they put it on its stand, and it gives light to everyone in the house. In the same way, let your light shine before others, that they may see your good deeds and glorify your Father in heaven" (Matt. 5:14–16). Jesus is counting on us, His followers, to be His hands and feet to redeem this lost world. He calls us to draw our lost neighbors and friends into the light of Christ. There is no plan B; we are it! If the magnitude of this calling causes you to fall on your knees, then you are right where Jesus wants you to be—humble and trusting Him to work in and through your life. He is looking to work through your church as well.

According to a 2022 Barna Research poll, only 42 percent of Christians in the United States believe being on mission is a biblical mandate.[40] That means the majority of those who claim Christ as their Lord don't see themselves as agents of His mission charged to enlarge His kingdom. May this never be any of us! It is a privilege to witness to others, serve the poor, and meet the needs of the homeless, along with the thousands of other ways God might use you to further His kingdom. There is no role too small and no vision too great. Serving may push you out of your comfort zone, but what an exciting place to be!

Throughout recorded history, people have been content to spend their lives chasing the accumulation of wealth and stuff, thinking this might cause some level of happiness. This quest is futile and won't succeed because what is actually sought is the joy and peace only found in God. The story of the rich man and Lazarus introduces us to a man who spent his life chasing wealth only to find it left him empty and distant from God. He realized when he died that he had lived for the wrong things and was in torment because it was too late to turn back (Luke 16:19–31). Don't spend your life squandering your resources of time, money, and attention on the wrong things.

The second of the Ten Commandments isn't talked about much today: you shall not make idols (Exod. 20:4). The next verse further explains this command, stating, "You shall not bow down to them or worship them; for I, the LORD your God, am a jealous God" (v. 5a). I doubt many of us struggle with worshipping little statues or trinkets we believe have supernatural powers, but the principle driving this command is that our heart, the center of our lives, is built to be inhabited by the Holy Spirit. He is to be our primary source of joy, occupation, and seeking. Whenever we invest more emotional energy in the pursuit of lesser life endeavors at the expense of our first love, then we are actually guilty of idolatry.

Consider for a moment what *good* things you are pursuing that have the potential to push God into the cheap seats. There is nothing wrong, in and of itself, with money, vacations, promotions, influence, sporting events, power, or status. These are noble things when used for God's glory. But when we invest our energies in these, believing they will fulfill us, more than we invest in our relationship with Jesus and His mission, then we are missing out. We may be focusing more on the *objects* of our blessings rather than the *Source* of our blessings.

A well-intentioned, aggressive mindset often nets earthly rewards. A kingdom mindset nets eternal rewards. Earthly pursuits aren't in themselves wrong but must be approached with the mind of Jesus, guided by His morals, and viewed through a kingdom lens.

If we have received Christ's gift of abundant life purchased on the cross, then He owns all of us—our time, treasure, hobbies, and relationships. Every investment of time, money, or resources should be run through the filter of whether or not it is a God-honoring endeavor. In light of eternity, our time here on the earth is like a short sneeze. Let's invest now to bless and to lead in response to what Jesus has done for us.

Discuss and Reflect

1. How do you feel about being on God's team and being an ambassador for Christ in this world?

2. When have you seen the Lord use you to touch someone else's life? How did that make you feel?

3. In Luke 9:23, Jesus said this to His disciples, "Whoever wants to be my disciple must deny themselves and take up their cross daily and follow me." Are you willing to stand up and be counted as one of Jesus's followers?

4. What are you living for: this temporary life or eternal life?

5. How would you define the Old Testament term *idolatry*?

16

How Do I Live This New Life?

As has been said, following Jesus is not a religion, it is a relationship. When Jesus invited His earliest disciples to "Come, follow me, and I will send you out to fish for men" (Matt. 4:19), He was not inviting them to a single event but an engagement for life, and for all eternity. Jesus was gracious to give us some pictures of what living our new life might look like with Him.

The salvation Jesus offers us is a process with three distinct phases:

> 1. Phase 1 is our **justification**. When Jesus hung on the cross for our sins and cried out, "It is finished" (John 19:30), our sin penalty was paid in full. Therefore, we have been justified before God—just-as-if we had never sinned. Our sins were forgiven and forgotten.

2. Now that we have been grafted into God's family, phase 2 of salvation begins. This is called **sanctification,** which is the process of putting off our old self and old ways of life and putting on the characteristics of Jesus. Now that we know Jesus, we are drawn to become more and more like Him, with the help of the Holy Spirit, of course! In this phase we work diligently to enjoy Jesus and grow in our understanding of him.

3. We remain in this second phase until we die and go to heaven. That is when we experience the third and final phase of our salvation called **glorification**. This is when we arrive to perfect righteousness, like that of Jesus, completely free from any traces of sinful behavior. We spend eternity in this glorified state.

How can we participate with the Spirit in our sanctification? Years ago, the Navigator's ministry developed this wheel illustration[41] to give Christians a vision for what is essential for rolling forward in our faith.

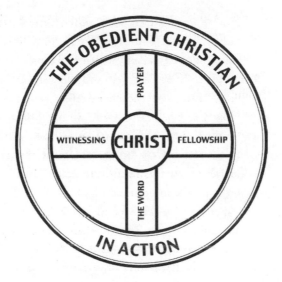

The hub—at the center of the wheel is Christ. Everything else will flow from this central, core relationship.

The two vertical spokes address our communication with God. The upward vertical spoke is *prayer*. Jesus is excited about every aspect of our lives and wants to be in conversation with us each day. We are encouraged to bring our praises and petitions to Him often (Heb 13:15).

The downward vertical spoke is *The Word*. The Bible teaches us important doctrines that serve as a road map for godly living. Even more, the Bible is God's love letter to us. He speaks to us through His Word in very practical ways. There is wisdom and discernment there for making decisions. This is why I strongly suggest making a daily practice of reading God's Word.

The two horizontal spokes address our relationships with other people. It is important we have *fellowship* with other believers who can encourage us in our journey. Church is important for this reason. Being in a small group Bible study or meeting with a friend for accountability are great investments as well.

Witnessing is how our faith is seen by those who don't know Jesus. The apostle Paul says, "We are to God the pleasing aroma of Christ among those who are being saved and those who are perishing" (2 Cor. 2:15). Just as Jesus shared the gift of salvation with us, we have the privilege to pass it along to those in our circle of influence. In fact, Jesus's final words to the onlookers at His ascension was the famous Great Commission: "Therefore go and make disciples of all nations, baptizing them in the name of the Father and of the Son and of the Holy Spirit, and teaching them to obey everything I have commanded you. And surely I am with you always, to the very end of the age" (Matt. 28:19–20).

The Lord has called us to spread the good news and reproduce the faith given to us. What greater gift could you give a family member or friend than an introduction to eternal life through Jesus? What a privilege!

Finally, the rim that holds the wheel together is *obedience to Christ*. If we believe in Jesus, then we trust what he says is true, right, and best for all involved. Therefore, we strive to put into practice what He says, and we work to avoid letting temptations in the world keep us from doing as God has commanded. Jesus said to His disciples, "I have told you these things, so that in me you may have peace. In this world you will have trouble. But take heart! I have overcome the world" (John 16:33).

Here are a few proven practices to assist you in building your own personal growth plan:

1. Learn to feed yourself spiritually. Develop the habit of a quiet time where you:
   - Read the Bible, seeking to understand what is written.
   - Connect with the Lord in prayer and cover your sphere of influence in prayer (1 Sam. 12:23).

2. Engage with peers for encouragement. Find a friend or group of friends who would like to pursue Christ together. Share what you are learning, read through a devotional for a month together, and so forth.

3. Pursue mission and service. A sense of mission helps form a kingdom perspective. There are any number of opportunities to volunteer based on your gifts and skills. Jesus said, "For even the Son of Man did not come to be served, but to serve, and to give his life as a ransom for many" (Mark 10:45).

4. Be an active member of a local church. The Lord has called us into His family, the church. It is the intended home for every believer for their long-term thriving.

5. Seek to multiply your faith. Second Timothy 2:2 challenges every follower of Jesus to intentionally invest in others who will, in turn, lead others to Christ. Most new believers see themselves as too immature spiritually to impact the life of another, or even share their testimony. But the challenge to do so presses them to dependence on the Holy Spirit and to walk more faithfully with the Lord.

Why Do We Need the Church?

Sadly, the church has a somewhat strained reputation these days. People looking in from the outside miss the heart of the church and instead only see issues upon which they disagree. As believers become more persecuted by society at large, it is important we band together to encourage our highest priorities. Listen to what God's Word says about His church:

- Jesus established the church: "Although I hope to come to you soon, I am writing you these instructions so that, if I am delayed, you will know how people ought to conduct themselves in God's household, which is the church of the living God, the pillar and foundation of the truth" (1 Tim. 3:14–15). What do pillars do? How important are foundations? I think the point here is clear.

- His people, His church, are called to worship: "Praise the LORD! Praise God in his sanctuary; praise him in his mighty heavens! Praise him for his mighty deeds; praise him according to his excellent greatness! . . . Let everything that has breath praise the LORD! Praise the LORD!" (Ps. 150:1–2, 6 ESV). Worship happens both individually, and collectively as the church.

- We are one body: Paul uses the metaphor of the body in 1 Corinthians 12 to emphasize that individual Christians need to be connected to other individual Christians. Head, shoulders, knees, and toes—they all depend on each other: "But in fact God has placed the parts in the body, every one of them, just as he wanted them to be. If they were all one part, where would the body be? As it is, there are many parts, but one body" (1 Cor. 12:18–20).

- Within the church we discover our gifts. LeBron James didn't know he had basketball talent until he played the game with others. There is a role for each of us in the church, and it lacks if we aren't involved.

- Being with fellow believers gives us strength to stand firm in a fallen world (1 Cor. 15:58).

He is like a vine, and we are like branches on that vine. If we disconnect, we die.

- The effectiveness of our witness depends on our love for one another. The church is called to be the "light of the world" (Matt. 5:14). We must be a united force for that light to prevail. After the Last Supper, Jesus shed fresh light on an old command. He told His disciples, "I give you a new commandment, that you love one another. Just as I have loved you, you also should love one another. By this everyone will know that you are my disciples, if you have love for one another" (John 13:34–35 NRSVA). In other words, our love for our fellow believers is the calling card that causes friends outside of the faith to be attracted to Jesus.

The Most Valuable Habit to Cultivate

Allow me to close this chapter with what I hope will be a special gift. Following my introduction to Jesus as a high school student, my Young Life leader encouraged me to begin reading the Bible and introduced me to the concept of a "quiet time." While I was motivated to get to know my newfound Savior, the habit of a daily meeting with the Lord eluded me until I had the privilege to serve on the work crew at Young Life's Saranac Village for a month. There, our bosses sent us out alone each morning armed with a Bible and notebook to meet with the Lord. These times were sweet, and the camaraderie of a group of peers all pursuing Christ together spurred me on!

When I joined the Young Life staff at age twenty-four, my boss, Chuck Reinhold, informed his regional staff that he wanted to give us a gift. We thought we might receive gift cards to a trendy restaurant, but no! The gift was a challenge to commit to beginning each of the next ninety days with an hour of Scripture reading and prayer, listening to the Lord for applications. If any one of us missed a day, we would all have to start the ninety days over again, so as you can imagine, accountability was high! While it took our group more than ninety days to complete the challenge, we did it, and through the process, the most life-transforming habit anyone can acquire was established in me!

It should never cease to amaze us that the Creator of the universe, the Author and Perfecter of our Faith, the One who assigns purpose and meaning to our lives, pledges to be with us always and stands ready to offer guidance for every aspect of our lives. "Here I am! I stand at the door and knock. If anyone hears my voice and opens the door, I will come in and eat with that person, and they with me" (Rev. 3:20).

Consider the benefits afforded us in a time of quiet with the Lord. We experience a personal touch of His love—not just for all mankind, but for us individually. We are assured of His forgiveness and favor. We glean from His eternal perspective. We gain vision, wisdom, and discernment for the activities before us. And we connect with His heart in prayer as we intercede for those in our sphere of influence. Why would we ever miss such a privileged encounter? Psalm 1 assures us of this: "Blessed is the man . . . [whose] delight is in the law of the LORD, and on his law he meditates day and night. He is like a tree planted by streams of water that yields its fruit in its season, and its leaf does not wither. In all that he does, he prospers" (vv. 1–3 ESV).

I recently heard an interesting insight into the encounter Moses had with God in the burning bush. Moses decided to pay attention to this unusual occurrence—"*he turned aside to see*" (Exod. 3:4 ESV)—and by so doing was determined to explore what it might hold for his life. It was in response to Moses's initiative to turn toward God that the Lord spoke to him "as a man speaks with his friend" (Exod. 33:11 CSB). What might "turning aside" to hear from the Lord look like for us? Answer: *Giving Him the priority of our first meeting every day.*

Jesus Modeled His Own Need for Regular Solitude with His Father

Here are two pictures the Scriptures afford us: "Very early in the morning, while it was still dark, Jesus got up, left the house and went off to a solitary place, where he prayed" (Mark 1:35). Do you think He may have been tired from the rigors of His schedule? Do you think He could have used some extra time in the morning to prepare for His day, or maybe just read a book to relax? Sure! But He knew that nothing was as important as His relationship with His Father and the insights He might glean for the myriad of encounters the day would hold. Should that not be true of us? Which of these excuses trumps our need to be with the Lord?

"I'm not a morning person."

"If I don't work out in the morning, I won't get to it."

"I'm on kid duty in the morning."

"I have to leave for school or work too early and need my sleep."

"I feel like I'm just checking the box, not actually meeting with Jesus."

"I don't think about what I read during my quiet time the rest of the day, so why bother?"

The second picture comes from Jesus's temptation in the wilderness. When tempted by the devil for forty days, Jesus relied on God's Word to focus, strengthen, and assure Him so that He did not succumb: "Man shall not live on bread alone, but on every word that comes from the mouth of God" (Matt. 4:4). The only way to live obediently and to rise above the temptations all around us is to draw strength and perspective from the Author of Life on a daily basis.

The Key to a Life of Flourishing

In John 15, we find Jesus with His disciples in a vineyard just hours before His arrest and crucifixion. He used the image of grapevines and branches to hammer home the key to a flourishing life or, as He phrased it, "bear[ing] fruit that will be lasting" (v. 16 PHILLIPS). What was this key? Eleven times in seventeen verses, Jesus used the word *abide*, which means to stay with continually, to make one's home. "As the branch cannot bear fruit by itself, unless it abides in the vine, neither can you, unless you abide in me" (John 15:4b ESV). Everything in the grapevine flows naturally to the branches. The riches of the Lord are at our disposal as we abide in Him.

A Few Suggestions for Energizing Your Quiet Times

1. *Begin with praise and thanksgiving* for His goodness to you, and the opportunity to sit with Him personally.
2. *Follow a reading plan.* There is consistency and flow in most every book of the Bible. Just opening to any random page feels haphazard.
3. *Develop a written prayer strategy* that honors the people and priorities in your life. "As for me, far be it from me that I should sin against

the LORD by failing to pray for you" (1 Sam. 12:23a).

4. Whenever possible, *look for an application* and write it down—something you can put into practice that causes you to walk with Jesus during your day. This implies keeping a journal, either handwritten or electronic. "Hearing a word from God is anything but a passive enterprise."[42]

5. *Find a friend to walk with* and share how you're doing and what you're learning, and to pray for one another. "And let us consider how we may spur one another on toward love and good deeds, not giving up meeting together, as some are in the habit of doing, but encouraging one another" (Heb. 10:24–25a). The journey is more fun together!

Discuss and Reflect

1. What is the key to a life of flourishing?

2. How has God transformed your life through time in His Word? Have you come to rely on it, or is it easy to skip a quiet time?

3. What spiritual habits have you struggled to create? How might you seek to do so after reading this chapter?

4. Who might you join with to seek God together and provide accountability to one another?

CONCLUSION

Has Jesus Really Risen from the Dead?

In John 1 we read where John the Baptist was standing and talking with two of his disciples when Jesus walked by. John pointed to Jesus and said, "Look, the Lamb of God!" The two disciples heard him say this, and they followed Jesus. When Jesus turned and saw them following, he said to them, "What are you looking for?" (John 1:35–38a csb).

What are we really looking for in life? The majority of people around us may not fully grasp what and who they truly seek is Jesus of Nazareth. In Him, we find the living, personal God; absolute truth; and our purpose in life. In His church we find a community of faithful friends to encourage us and engage in mission together.

Allow me to finish my fraternity pledge kidnapping story I started in chapter 3.

I found a farmhouse with the light on and gently knocked on their door. The nice couple informed me I was only about a mile from campus and pointed the way back home. While their intervention came as quite a relief, it pales in comparison to the freedom and joy I feel having been set free from the weight of sin and its consequences.

I will be forever grateful to my friend Jenny, who invited me to my first Young Life club, which was my introduction to the idea of a personal relationship with Jesus and the freedom that He gives. I am truly a new creation: "The old has gone, the new is here!" (2 Cor. 5:17).

Between the death of Jesus and His resurrection, Luke imparts the experience of two disciples walking along the road to Emmaus. These men were, no doubt, discouraged and bewildered by the apparent death of their Lord. Jesus joins them on their walk but hides His identity until they break bread together that evening: "When he was at the table with them, he took bread, blessed and broke it, and gave it to them. Then their eyes were opened, and they recognized him; and he vanished from their sight. They said to each other, 'Were not our hearts burning within us while he was talking to us on the road, while he was opening the scriptures to us?'" (Luke 24:30–32 NRSVA).

When these two disciples return to the larger group they exclaim, "It is true! The Lord has risen . . ." (v. 34). Joy and amazement overtook these men because they saw that it was all true: Jesus is the Messiah. I pray this will be your result as well!

Taste and see that the LORD is good;
>   blessed is the one who takes refuge in him.
Fear the LORD, you his holy people,
>   for those who fear him lack nothing.
The lions may grow weak and hungry,
>   but those who seek the LORD lack no good
>   thing. . . .

The eyes of the LORD are on the righteous,
>   and his ears are attentive to their cry.
(Psalm 34:8–10, 15)

Discuss and Reflect

1. Who do you conclude Jesus is from the evidence presented?

2. What do you believe Jesus wants most for each one of us?

3. If it's all true, what response does this demand of you?

Notes

1. Alisa Childers, *Another Gospel* (Carol Stream, IL: Tyndale House, 2020), 10.

2. Dale Bruner, *The Gospel of John* (Grand Rapids, MI: Eerdmans, 2012), 157.

3. Big Think Blog, "How to Find Fulfillment: Lessons from Dark Horse' Success," October 16, 2018, accessed April 23, 2023, https://www.youtube.com/watch?v=uhKlA4JjZvI.

4. Dictionary.com, "Success," accessed April 24, 2023, https://www.dictionary.com/browse/success.

5. "It Is Never Enough—Wealthy People Desire Money and Status More Than Less Fortunate," Technology.org, September 26, 2019, accessed April 24, 2023.

6. Dhruv Khullar, "Finding Purpose for a Good Life but Also a Healthy One," *New York Times*, January 1, 2018, accessed April 25, 2023, https://www.nytimes.com/2018/01/01/upshot/finding-purpose-for-a-good-life-but-also-a-healthy-one.html.

7. This is a conflation of Ecclesiastes 8:15, Luke 12:19, Isaiah 22:13, and 1 Corinthians 15:32.

8. David King, "How Religion Motivates People to Give and Serve," *The Conversation*, August 19, 2017, accessed April 25, 2023, https://theconversation.com/how-religion-motivates-people-to-give-and-serve-81662.

9. Webstersdictionary.com, "Success," accessed April 24, 2023, https://webstersdictionary1828.com/Dictionary/truth.

10. Dr. Steven J. Lawson is founder and president of OnePassion Ministries in Dallas. It was originally posted in Table Talk from Ligoneer Ministries, September 1, 2010.

11. Jennifer Kavanaugh and Michael D. Rich, "Truth Decay," *Rand Corporation*, accessed April 24, 2023, https://www.rand.org/pubs/research_reports/RR2314.html.

12. Lindy Keffer, "Absolute Truth in a Relativistic World," *Focus on the Family*, April 2019, 1.

13. Tim Keller, "The Decline and Renewal of the American Church: Part 4—The Strategy for Renewal," Life in the Gospel, accessed April 25, 2023, https://bit.ly/AmericanChurch_Part4.

14. Llana Horwitz, "I Followed the Lives of 3,290 Teenagers. This Is What I Learned About Religion and Education," *New York Times*, Opinion Guest Essay, March 15, 2022, accessed April 25, 2023, https://www.nytimes.com/2022/03/15/opinion/religion-school-success.html.

15. James Emery White, "That's Just Your Interpretation," Church and Culture Blog, March 24, 2022, accessed April 25, 2023, https://www.churchandculture.org/blog/2022/3/24/thats-just-your-interpretation.

16. Ken Boa and Larry Moody, *I'm Glad You Asked: In-Depth Answers to Difficult Questions about Christianity* (Colorado Springs, CO: David C. Cook Publishing, 1982), 92.

17. Boa and Moody, *I'm Glad You Asked*, 93.

18. Boa and Moody, *I'm Glad You Asked*.

19. Bert Thompson and Wayne Jackson, *The Case for the Existence of God* (Montgomery, AL: Apologetics Press, 1996), 20.

20. Thompson and Jackson, *The Case for the Existence of God*, 20.

21. *Science Digest*, 1981, 89[1]:124, Hearst Brand Development.

22. Thompson and Jackson, *The Case for the Existence of God*, 20.

23. Thompson and Jackson, *The Case for the Existence of God*, 21.

24. Thompson and Jackson, *The Case for the Existence of God*, 22.

25. George Gaylord Simpson, *The Meaning of Life* (New Haven, CT: Yale University Press, 1949), 293.

26. Thompson and Jackson, *The Case for the Existence of God*, 25.

27. Thompson and Jackson, *The Case for the Existence of God*, 27.

28. Apologetic Press, "The Earth–Our 'Just Right' Planet," Apologetics Press Kids, August 10, 2010, accessed April 25, 2023, https://apologeticspress.org/the-earthour-just-right-planet-3359/.

29. Jaroslav Pelikan, *Jesus Through the Centuries: His Place in the History of Culture* (New Haven, CT: Yale University Press, 1985), 8.

30. C. S. Lewis, *Mere Christianity* (New York: Simon and Schuster, 1980), 56.

31. Young Writers Award, "The Dash Poem—Linda Ellis," accessed May 24, 2023, https://youngwritersaward.com.au/the-dash-poem-linda-ellis/.

32. Bruner, *The Gospel of John*, xvi.

33. Tim Keller, *The Reason for God: Belief in an Age of Skepticism* (New York: Penguin Books), 2009.

34. Wilbur M. Smith, *A Great Certainty in This Hour of World Crises* (Wheaton, IL: Van Kampen Press, 1951), 10–11.

35. Josephus, *Antiquities* 18.63–64, cited in Edwin M. Yamauchi, "Jesus Outside the New Testament: What Is the Evidence?," in *Jesus Under Fire: Modern Scholarship Reinvents the Historical Jesus* (Grand Rapids, MI: Zondervan, 1995), 212.

36. Chris Goswami, "Why Does God Allow Bad Things to Happen?," *Baptists Times*, April 30, 2019, accessed April 25, 2023, https://www.baptist.org.uk/Articles/547266/Why_does_God.aspx.

37. Timothy George, ed., *J. I. Packer and the Evangelical Future: The Impact of His Life and Thought* (Grand Rapids, MI: Baker Academic, 2009), 253.

38. *The Bridge to Life* © 1969 by The Navigators. Used by permission. All rights reserved.

39. Walter Pavlo, "Character Is What You Do When EVERYONE Is Watching," *Forbes* magazine, October 23, 2012, accessed April 25,

2023, https://www.forbes.com/sites/walterpavlo/2012/10/23/character-is-what-you-do-when-everyone-is-watching/?sh=5c42ea65fc6d.

40. Barna Group, "Pastors See Missions as a Mandate, but Christians Aren't So Sure," Barna Research, April 20, 2022, accessed April 25, 2023, https://www.barna.com/research/missions-mandate/.

41. *The Wheel* © 1976 by The Navigators. Used by permission. All rights reserved.

42. James Emery White, "Why Hearing from God Is Not a Passive Exercise," *Outreach Magazine*, August 1, 2019, https://outreachmagazine.com/features/discipleship/45016-why-hearing-from-god-is-not-a-passive-exercise.html.